Leveraging Artificial Intelligence to Transform Teacher Education Accreditation

Leveraging Artificial Intelligence to Transform Teacher Education Accreditation

A Framework for Innovation and Equity

Anne Tapp Jaksa, Beth Kubitskey, Malina Monoco, and Joey Pearson

Foreword by Yuhang Rong

BLOOMSBURY ACADEMIC
NEW YORK · LONDON · OXFORD · NEW DELHI · SYDNEY

BLOOMSBURY ACADEMIC
Bloomsbury Publishing Inc, 1359 Broadway, New York, NY 10018, USA
Bloomsbury Publishing Plc, 50 Bedford Square, London, WC1B 3DP, UK
Bloomsbury Publishing Ireland, 29 Earlsfort Terrace, Dublin 2, D02 AY28, Ireland

BLOOMSBURY, BLOOMSBURY ACADEMIC and the Diana logo are trademarks
of Bloomsbury Publishing Plc

First published in the United States of America 2026

Cover design by Kathi Ha
Cover images © iStock.com/Anueing and watchara_tongnoi

Library of Congress Cataloging-in-Publication Data is available

ISBN: HB: 979-8-2163-7521-0
PB: 979-8-2163-7517-3
ePDF: 979-8-2163-7518-0
eBook: 979-8-2163-7519-7

Typeset by Deanta Global Publishing Services, Chennai, India
Printed and bound in the United States of America

For product safety related questions contact productsafety@bloomsbury.com.

To find out more about our authors and books visit www.bloomsbury.com and
sign up for our newsletters.

For Joe, my partner in life and learning, whose work in criminal justice exemplifies the balance of ethics and innovation reflected in this book. —Anne

For Dean Emeritus Jerry Robbins, whose lifelong commitment to educator preparation and innovation continues to inspire, and for my husband, Mark, whose steadfast support made this journey possible. —Beth

For all the assessment and accreditation coordinators, herders of cats, gatherers of data, and champions of continuous improvement driving innovation in educator preparation. —Malina

For Dr. Emily Feistritzer, founder of Moreland University, who believed in me and opened the door for me to step into my calling at a young age and for the Moreland faculty and staff whose dedication to preparing teachers continues to inspire me. —Joey

Contents

Online Resources

Appendix B provides suggested prompts that readers can use to begin using AI to develop their own quality assurance system for continuous improvement (and accreditation). These are just suggestions as a starting point, as everyone's AI journey is unique. Try it yourself and see. Appendix B can be accessed on the book's companion website at Bloomsbury.pub/leveragingai.

Foreword

As institutions of higher education navigate the accelerating pace of technological and societal change, the evolution of accreditation processes represents both a remarkable opportunity and a profound responsibility. Accreditation has been a unique mechanism in American higher education. It has long been a cornerstone of educational quality assurance, built upon standards established by content and field experts, shaped through demonstrated research outcomes, and upheld by peer review. It is a structured, yet evolving mechanism guided by the central question: *How do we know that our students have learned and can practice what the programs intend for them to learn and practice?* This process reflects a commitment to excellence, transparency, and accountability.

Historically, accreditation has involved retrospective evidence, manual data collection, and time-intensive documentation. Today, this process is shifting toward a more dynamic, data-informed cycle of reflection, alignment, and strategic improvement. Emerging tools and systems are helping institutions manage complexity, streamline reporting, and strengthen the link between educational outcomes and continuous improvement. What was once primarily a compliance exercise is becoming an opportunity for deeper institutional storytelling and evidence-based growth.

Yet, as we embrace innovation, we must proceed with discernment. Education is not a process of training robots. It is about cultivating human potential—minds and hearts with moral standards, with critical thinking skills to raise questions, to adapt knowledge and skills into real-world contexts, and to possess the curiosity to discover new ideas and phenomena. Accreditation processes are valuable precisely because they help institutions tell their unique stories of student success. Any tools we use—technological or otherwise—must serve this human-centered mission.

Over the last twenty-plus years engaged in accreditation, I have had the fortune to work with dedicated educators. Drs. Tapp Jaska, Kubitskey, Monaco, and Pearson are among those who are deeply committed to academic quality and to preparing future generations with the knowledge, skills, and dispositions to make the world a better place. Their collaboration in this book, *Leveraging Artificial Intelligence to Transform Teacher Education Accreditation: A Framework for Innovation and Equity*, offers a timely and necessary exploration of how educator preparation programs can embrace innovation while remaining grounded in values of equity, rigor, and professional integrity.

The scenarios, frameworks, and reflective prompts provided in this book will be invaluable to institutional leaders, faculty, and accreditors working to strengthen the evaluative practices that define high-quality teacher education. At its heart, this work reminds us that improvement is not simply about automation or efficiency—but about thoughtful, ethical, and principled engagement with the systems we build to support student learning and professional preparation.

If there is a single takeaway, it is this: innovation should not be seen as a replacement for the professional wisdom that educators and accreditors bring to the table. Rather, it should be cultivated as a partner—an amplifier of human insight, a catalyst for strategic reflection, and a safeguard for the values that define the teaching profession.

Yuhang Rong, Ph.D.
Chair, Board of Directors, Council for the Accreditation of Educator Preparation
Associate Vice President Emeritus, University of Connecticut
Strategic Advisor for North America, Kaplan International Pathways

Preface

The writing of this book reflects both tradition and innovation. As accreditation experts, we drew on decades of collective experience in educator preparation and quality assurance. At the same time, we engaged with emerging technologies to support our writing process. Portions of the editing were supported by the use of Artificial Intelligence tools, specifically OpenAI's ChatGPT and Grammarly. These tools were employed for brainstorming, generating language, and refining prose. Importantly, all content was reviewed, verified, and revised by the authors. We emphasize that we are accreditation professionals working with currently available technology—not AI programmers or technical specialists. The role of AI here was practical and supportive, always grounded in our professional expertise and ultimate responsibility for the final work.

This book also represents a first step in a larger and ongoing conversation about the integration of AI into accreditation. We recognize that the pace of change in AI is extraordinarily rapid. What feels innovative and useful today may, within a short time, appear limited, outdated, or even obsolete. As these tools evolve, so too will the ethical standards, best practices, and expectations for their responsible use in academic and professional contexts. Readers should understand this book as both a reflection of our expertise and a snapshot of this particular moment in time.

The history of accreditation shows that innovation is always disruptive, often messy, and inevitably transformative. A striking example comes from Eastern Michigan University (EMU) in 1997, when Dean Emeritus Jerry Robbins led EMU's pioneering effort in NCATE's first-ever "paperless" accreditation review. With faculty, staff, and administrators working late nights over a summer, shelves of paper evidence were painstakingly retyped, cleaned, and posted to a rudimentary website. Connectivity was limited, "sneaker net" transfers carried diskettes across campus, and some reviewers still demanded boxes of paper. Yet this experiment created a national precedent: reviewers accessed evidence remotely, interviews were conducted electronically, and the accreditation process itself began to shift toward digital formats (Robbins, n.d.).

Robbins's lesson—that innovation in accreditation requires courage, cultural change, and a willingness to build systems before policies exist—resonates strongly today. Just as EMU had to digitize, clean, and organize its evidence base before a digital review was possible, educator preparation programs now face the challenge of preparing their data ecosystems before AI can add real value. Then, as now, issues of training, equity, governance, and human oversight remained central. The groundwork laid by EMU for digital reviews parallels today's transition to AI: both remind us that transformative change in accreditation is never just technical—it is cultural, ethical, and deeply human.

Our aim is not to provide the definitive word on AI and accreditation but to chart a path forward—one that acknowledges the potential of AI while remaining attentive to its limitations, ethical implications, and the irreplaceable role of human judgment. In this spirit, we invite readers to approach the chapters ahead as both a reflection of lessons learned and an invitation to help shape the next chapter of innovation in accreditation.

1 Artificial Intelligence's Role in Teacher Education Accreditation and Continuous Improvement

Introduction

Note to the Reader: *Throughout this book, recurring themes include the essential role of human engagement, the reminder that AI is a tool, not a replacement, and a focus on ethical practice. This repetition is intentional. These values are foundational to accreditation work and must remain at the forefront of any discussion of AI integration. Just as continuous improvement depends on cycles of reflection, so too does this book revisit these principles to emphasize their enduring importance.*

Accreditation is the bedrock of quality assurance in educator preparation, ensuring that teacher education programs maintain high standards of professional and ethical practice. Over the last decade, expectations for educator preparation programs (EPPs) have escalated in response to shifting policy mandates, workforce needs, and dynamic educational contexts (CAEP, 2022; Zawacki-Richter et al., 2019). Accrediting organizations such as the Council for the Accreditation of Educator Preparation (CAEP) require robust, data-driven evidence demonstrating candidate competence, equitable outcomes, and institutional commitment to continuous improvement (Salas-Pilco et al., 2022). Yet, traditional accreditation workflows—often characterized by static reporting cycles, fragmented data systems, and resource-intensive documentation—are increasingly unsuited to meet these complex demands (Zawacki-Richter et al., 2019) (See Table 1.1).

Addressing these challenges requires innovative approaches that can enhance efficiency without compromising academic rigor or equity. Artificial Intelligence (AI), although not a replacement for human judgment, offers transformative potential for modernizing accreditation practices. When thoughtfully implemented, AI can improve data integrity, streamline compliance processes, uncover systemic inequities, and promote institutional innovation (Holmes & Porayska-Pomsta, 2023). This chapter establishes foundational concepts and explores how AI may reshape accreditation, positioning it not merely as a compliance exercise but as a catalyst for continuous improvement and educational equity.

Table 1.1 Traditional Versus AI-Enhanced Accreditation Workflow

Step	Traditional Workflow	AI-Enhanced Workflow
Data Collection	Manual entry, siloed systems	Automated data aggregation
Evidence Mapping	Faculty interpretations	Natural language processing tools
Compliance Review	Delayed, subjective	Real-time dashboards, predictive alerts
Report Generation	Time-intensive writing	AI-assisted drafting
Equity Monitoring	Infrequent and anecdotal	Equity dashboards, disaggregated analytics

The Evolution of Accreditation in Educator Preparation

Historically, accreditation in teacher education was driven by state-level compliance, focusing heavily on procedural documentation rather than outcomes (CAEP, 2022). A pivotal shift occurred with the 2013 merger of the National Council for Accreditation of Teacher Education (NCATE) and the Teacher Education Accreditation Council (TEAC) into CAEP, which introduced evidence-based and outcomes-focused standards. This realignment required EPPs to produce longitudinal data on candidate performance, disaggregate results by demographic subgroups, and demonstrate institutional learning from accreditation feedback (Salas-Pilco et al., 2022) (See Figure 1.1).

The Case for AI in Accreditation

Artificial Intelligence is particularly well-suited to address the inefficiencies of traditional accreditation processes. AI systems excel at ingesting vast quantities of data, detecting subtle patterns, and delivering timely, actionable insights (See Table 1.2). AI tools—when guided by human expertise—can:

- Automate evidence mapping to accreditation standards.
- Identify performance gaps in candidate outcomes and program effectiveness.
- Enable predictive modeling to anticipate compliance risks.
- Support dynamic feedback loops for faculty development and program refinement (Salas-Pilco et al., 2022; Kasneci et al., 2023).

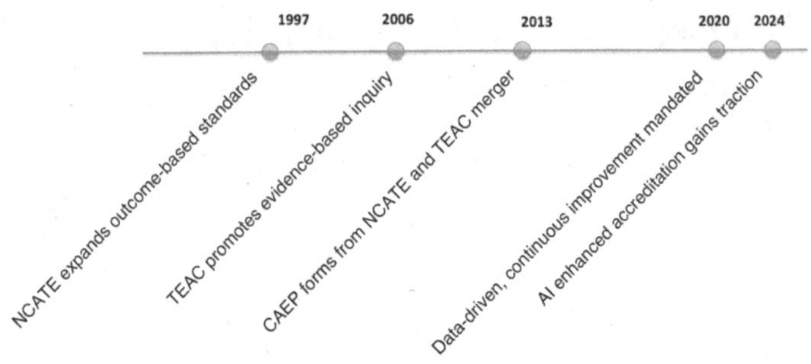

Figure 1.1 Accreditation evaluation timeline.

Table 1.2 AI Tools by Accreditation Task Matrix

Accreditation Task	AI Tools/Techniques
Evidence Collection	Machine learning, data scraping
Report Drafting	Generative AI (e.g., GPT)
Equity Monitoring	Learning analytics, bias detection
Program Evaluation	Predictive analytics, NLP
Feedback Mechanisms	AI chatbots, adaptive surveys

Beyond general benefits, several specific AI technologies are directly applicable to accreditation processes:

- Natural Language Processing (NLP): Enables automated analysis of accreditation narratives, stakeholder survey comments, and qualitative data from program evaluations (Salas-Pilco et al., 2022).

- Predictive Analytics: Supports forecasting program compliance risks, candidate performance, and resource needs (Mhlanga, 2023).

- Machine Learning Classification Models: Can detect subtle patterns in student success data or program outcomes, guiding targeted interventions.

- Learning Analytics Dashboards: Provide real-time visualizations for faculty and administrators to track key accreditation indicators (Prinsloo et al., 2021).

Such technologies move accreditation processes beyond static reporting cycles toward dynamic, data-driven continuous improvement.

AI and the Self-Study

An essential area where AI demonstrates transformative potential is the preparation of self-study reports required for accreditation. Traditionally, self-studies demand extensive narrative writing, evidence mapping, and data analysis—all time-consuming and resource-intensive tasks for faculty and accreditation staff.

Emerging research illustrates how AI tools such as generative language models and natural language processing can support these processes. For example, AI systems can support each of the following accreditation tasks:

- Draft preliminary sections of self-study reports based on accreditation standards and historical data (Kelly & Smith, 2024).
- Automatically map institutional evidence to relevant accreditation criteria (Homes et al., 2019).
- Summarize qualitative data from surveys, interviews, and program assessments to highlight key findings for accreditation narratives.

In this human-led approach, AI serves as a cognitive and organizational aid—streamlining routine documentation tasks while ensuring faculty remain the authors of record and ultimate decision-makers. By reducing administrative burdens,

AI enables academic teams to concentrate on higher-order work such as strategic reflection, program innovation, and evidence-based improvement.

Challenges in Traditional Accreditation

Despite significant advances in digital reporting, data-informed decision-making, and alignment with rigorous national standards, many EPPs remain constrained by persistent challenges that AI may help alleviate:

- Fragmented Data Systems: Disparate databases and software platforms impede comprehensive, integrated analysis (Zawacki-Richter et al., 2019).

- Delayed Feedback Loops: Traditional accreditation cycles produce static reports, hindering timely interventions (Mhlanga, 2023).

- Subjectivity and Inconsistency: Human interpretation of complex standards can introduce variability and bias into accreditation judgments (Zawacki-Richter et al., 2019).

- Documentation Overload: The preparation of evidence-heavy self-studies diverts faculty time from instructional and research priorities (Mhlanga, 2023).

These limitations prevent accreditation from fully realizing its potential as a mechanism for continuous quality improvement and systemic equity. Moreover, human cognition, while powerful, is inherently limited in its ability to process vast and complex datasets and is shaped by the bounds of individual lived experience. Artificial Intelligence can serve as a cognitive partner—extending analytic reach across broader contexts, enabling more nuanced pattern recognition, and augmenting our collective capacity for reflective thinking and critical analysis.

AI for Continuous Improvement and Equity

One of AI's most significant contributions lies in fostering real-time, data-informed continuous improvement. Through learning analytics, natural language processing, and predictive modeling, AI enables EPPs to detect trends, forecast risks, and target program interventions (Salas-Pilco et al., 2022; Kasneci et al., 2023).

Crucially, AI also serves as a powerful tool for advancing diversity, equity, and inclusion (DEI). As Zawacki-Richter et al. (2019) and Susanti (2025) emphasize, equity-focused AI can be strategically deployed to identify disparities across race, socioeconomic status, gender, and geographic region, thereby guiding resource allocation and policy interventions. Such capacity ensures accreditation becomes not only a compliance exercise but also a mechanism for systemic change. Beyond institutional processes, AI offers new opportunities for collaboration and benchmarking across educator preparation programs, fostering shared accountability, cross-institutional learning, and the global dissemination of equity-focused best practices.

AI for Cross-Institutional Benchmarking

Another emerging application of AI in accreditation is facilitating comparisons of accreditation data across institutions. AI-powered benchmarking tools, when implemented as part of a human-centered process, can assist in the following critical accreditation tasks:

- Identify patterns and best practices among peer institutions.
- Highlight areas where programs excel or lag relative to national or state benchmarks.
- Foster collaborative improvement efforts among EPPs.

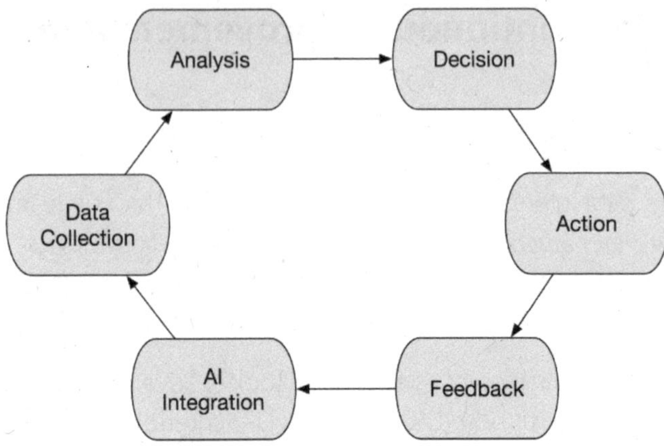

Figure 1.2 Continuous improvement loop with AI.

These comparative insights are especially valuable for programs seeking continuous improvement and innovation, and they align with calls for greater transparency and shared learning in accreditation practices (Mhlanga, 2023) (See Figure 1.2).

Importantly, AI's role in advancing equity hinges on rigorous bias detection and mitigation strategies. For instance:

- Bias audits of algorithms can uncover unintended disparities in recommendations or assessments (Popenici & Kerr, 2017).

- Fairness-aware machine learning techniques adjust model outputs to mitigate discriminatory effects.

- Data disaggregation by demographic factors enables targeted interventions to close equity gaps (Prinsloo et al., 2021; Salas-Pilco et al., 2022; U.S. Department of Education, 2023).

Without careful design and human oversight, AI tools risk replicating historical inequities rather than resolving them. Equity-focused AI implementation is therefore not optional—it is essential.

Ethical Considerations

Despite its transformative potential, AI in accreditation brings significant ethical and legal considerations (See Figure 1.3). Key issues include:

- Bias Mitigation: Algorithms must be regularly audited to prevent replicating or amplifying historical inequities (Popenici & Kerr, 2017).

- Data Privacy: Institutions must ensure compliance with regulations such as FERPA and GDPR to safeguard sensitive data (U.S. Department of Education, 2023).

- Transparency and Explainability: Stakeholders must understand how AI models generate outputs, particularly when decisions impact accreditation outcomes (Mhlanga, 2023).

- Faculty Autonomy: AI should be implemented as a support tool rather than as a replacement for professional judgment. Human-centered design must remain paramount.

Sustainable adoption of AI requires clear governance frameworks, professional development in AI literacy, and co-design processes involving faculty and accreditation stakeholders (Zawacki-Richter et al., 2019).

Implications for Practice

Based on an extensive review of the literature and case studies, several strategic human-centered strategies emerge for integrating AI into accreditation processes in ways that strengthen continuous improvement and advance equity:

- **Automated Data Management**: AI can streamline the collection, organization, and integration of accreditation evidence from multiple systems. By

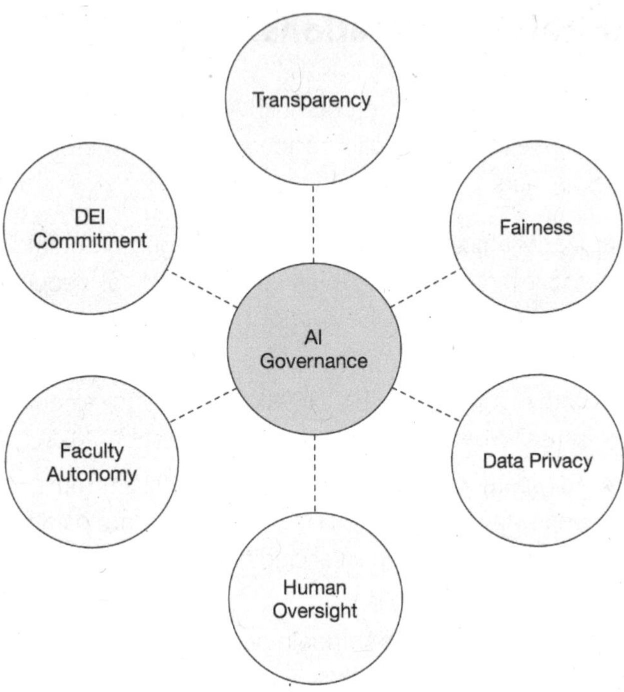

Figure 1.3 Ethical AI integration framework.

reducing manual data handling, faculty can dedicate more time to interpreting findings, identifying trends, and implementing targeted program improvements (Mhlanga, 2023).

- **Predictive Analytics for Risk Identification**: Machine learning models can flag early indicators of potential noncompliance or performance gaps, enabling proactive interventions before accreditation reviews. This predictive capacity supports a culture of continuous monitoring and adjustment rather than reactive problem-solving (Salas-Pilco et al., 2022).

- **Real-Time Feedback Systems**: AI dashboards can deliver immediate insights on candidate performance, faculty workload distribution, and program outcomes. These dynamic feedback loops allow institutions to test changes, assess impacts, and refine practices in shorter cycles, accelerating improvement efforts (Kasneci et al., 2023).

- **AI Literacy and Capacity-Building**: Equipping faculty, administrators, and reviewers with the skills to critically interpret AI outputs ensures that technology remains a tool for human-led decision-making rather than a determinant of it (U.S. Department of Education, 2023).

By embedding these strategies into a human-centered, cyclical review process, AI-enhanced accreditation shifts from a static, episodic evaluation to an ongoing, adaptive system of evidence-based decision-making. In this model, faculty and administrators remain the drivers of interpretation and action, while AI provides timely, integrated insights that inform reflection and planning. This continuous feedback loop enables educator preparation programs to respond quickly to policy changes, address emerging workforce needs, and advance equity goals—fostering sustained, systemic improvement rather than one-time compliance.

Illustrative Case Studies

Several recent studies showcase practical applications of AI in education that, while not exclusively focused on accreditation, provide insights relevant to teacher preparation programs:

- Kasneci et al. (2023) explored prompt engineering for large language models in educational contexts, demonstrating how structured and adaptive prompts can improve digital competencies critical for modern teaching and assessment practices. Their findings suggest that similar generative AI tools could support accreditation teams in drafting narrative reports, crafting evidence statements, and training faculty in writing aligned to accreditation standards.

- Li and Li (2025) implemented a personalized learning recommendation system using machine learning, demonstrating how predictive analytics can enhance individualized learning pathways—a concept transferable to program-level improvements and accreditation monitoring. For accreditation, such predictive tools could forecast program risks, identify areas needing improvement, and personalize institutional strategies to meet evolving accreditation criteria.

Together, these cases reveal how innovations tested in broader educational settings can be repurposed to make accreditation processes more adaptive, evidence-rich, and responsive—turning what has traditionally been a periodic compliance activity into a dynamic driver of program quality and equity.

Policy and Governance Recommendations

To fully realize the benefits of AI in accreditation while avoiding unintended harms, institutions and accrediting bodies must approach adoption with a deliberate, human-centered governance framework. This includes establishing clear boundaries for acceptable AI use, building capacity among stakeholders, and embedding safeguards to ensure that technology augments—rather than replaces—professional judgment. Key actions include:

- Developing clear policies defining acceptable AI use in accreditation documentation and decision-making.
- Investing in professional development to build AI literacy among faculty, administrators, and accreditation reviewers (U.S. Department of Education, 2023).
- Requiring transparency and explainability in AI models that influence accreditation decisions.
- Establishing mechanisms for ongoing audits of AI systems to detect and mitigate bias.
- Engaging faculty and stakeholders in co-designing AI solutions to ensure alignment with institutional values and priorities.

Such governance structures are crucial for maintaining public trust and ensuring that AI serves as a tool for enhancement rather than as a substitute for professional judgment.

Conclusion

The integration of Artificial Intelligence into teacher education accreditation marks a pivotal shift in how educational quality, accountability, and equity are pursued. While accreditation remains fundamentally a human-centered endeavor, AI offers powerful opportunities to reimagine its processes—leveraging vast datasets and advanced analytics to enable more efficient, insightful, and responsive approaches. Rather than simply easing reporting burdens, AI enhances the capacity of faculty and administrators to interpret data, identify systemic inequities, and act on evidence in real time.

When embedded in robust governance structures and guided by professional judgment, AI can transform accreditation from a periodic compliance activity into an ongoing, adaptive system for continuous improvement. Such systems not only keep pace with policy changes and workforce needs but also actively advance institutional equity goals. As Zawacki-Richter et al. (2019) and Susanti (2025) underscore, equity-driven AI has the potential to reshape accreditation into a living, reflective process that both meets rigorous standards and adapts to the complexities of modern education. Continued research, ethical oversight, and collaborative innovation will ensure that this transformation benefits all stakeholders and sustains the integrity of educator preparation.

Reflection Points

The following questions are designed to help educator preparation programs explore the foundational concepts, opportunities, and challenges of integrating Artificial Intelligence into accreditation. These questions encourage critical thinking about AI's potential to enhance efficiency, promote equity, and strengthen continuous improvement. They may be used for individual reflection, collaborative team discussions, or as part of strategic planning and professional development initiatives.

Evolving Accreditation

- How have recent changes in accreditation standards shifted the role of data in educator preparation programs?
- In what ways could AI help you respond to the increasing demand for disaggregated, equity-focused evidence?

AI as a Cognitive Partner

- Which aspects of your current accreditation process consume the most time and resources?

- How might AI tools, when guided by human expertise, help free up capacity for strategic reflection and improvement?

Continuous Improvement and Equity

- How could your program leverage AI to identify and address equity gaps in candidate performance?
- What safeguards would you need to put in place to ensure AI does not unintentionally reinforce bias?

Cross-Institutional Benchmarking

- What benefits and challenges might arise from comparing your accreditation data with peer institutions using AI tools?
- How could benchmarking insights be transformed into actionable strategies for program improvement?

Ethical and Governance Considerations

- What policies or governance structures would you need to develop before adopting AI for accreditation?
- How would you ensure transparency and faculty oversight in AI-assisted accreditation decisions?

Implications for Practice

- Which of the human-centered strategies outlined in this chapter could have the most immediate impact on your accreditation work?
- How might embedding AI into a cyclical review process change your institution's approach to continuous improvement?

Looking Ahead

- Based on the case studies provided, which AI applications feel most relevant to your context?

- How might your program pilot an AI tool while maintaining rigorous ethical oversight?

2 AI in Data-Driven Decision-Making for Accreditation

Introduction

AI is transforming the way EPPs engage with accreditation. Once a primarily cyclical process characterized by data gathering at fixed intervals, accreditation is increasingly becoming a dynamic, ongoing, and deeply data-driven practice. AI technologies offer tools for evidence collection, pattern recognition, predictive forecasting, and real-time decision support that allow institutions to shift from reactive compliance toward proactive quality assurance and innovation (Zawacki-Richter et al., 2019; U.S. Department of Education, 2023; UNESCO, 2021).

This evolution matters because accreditation is a central driver of educational quality, accountability, and public trust. The ability to collect, analyze, and act upon complex datasets in a timely, accurate, and ethical manner enables EPPs to demonstrate both compliance with existing standards and readiness for emerging expectations (Holmes et al., 2019; Williamson & Eynon, 2020).

Before we proceed any further, it's important to highlight the need for caution when using AI to analyze data and to ensure compliance with FERPA requirements regarding confidentiality. "A Quick Reference Guide: Using AI Tools Under FERPA" offers practical advice on how to utilize generative AI tools while adhering to the Family Educational Rights and Privacy Act (FERPA). You can find this guide in Appendix A, with key points summarized in Table 2.1.

Table 2.1 Quick Reference Guide: Using AI Tools Under FERPA

Do	Don't
Anonymize Data: Replace student names with codes (e.g., "Candidate A").	Upload Student Identifiers: Names, ID numbers, email addresses, or grades.
Use Aggregate Results: Summarize performance trends (e.g., "80 percent met standard").	Enter Identifiable Work: Lesson plans, assignments, or evaluations tied to specific students.
Draft with AI: Policies, rubrics, lesson plan templates, handbooks, accreditation reports.	Use AI for High-Stakes Decisions: Admissions, licensure, or final grading.
Generate Teaching Materials: Case studies, sample lessons, discussion prompts.	Store FERPA-Protected Records: Never upload to AI systems without IT/legal approval.
Use Institution-Approved Platforms: PreferEnterprise/Team accounts with administrative controls.	Assume AI is Confidential: Temporary chats help, but FERPA protections still apply.
Apply Human Oversight: Treat AI outputs as drafts—final evaluative judgment rests with faculty.	

Key Reminder
- FERPA protects any information that can identify a student.
- AI should be used as a decision-support tool, not as a record-keeping or compliance system.
- When uncertain, consult the institution's FERPA Officer before inputting data into AI systems.(OpenAI, 2025)

Episodes of Decision-Making in Accreditation

Accreditation is made up of numerous decision-making episodes, each with unique information requirements and stakes (U.S. Department of Education, 2023). These include:

1. **Annual Data Reviews**—Institutions examine trends in candidate performance, licensure pass rates, faculty qualifications, and placement outcomes.

2. **Mid-Cycle Evaluations**—Internal reviews that assess progress toward addressing prior recommendations and identify areas for enhancement.

3. **Targeted Improvement Plans**—Interventions designed in response to identified deficiencies or emerging challenges.

4. **Comprehensive Self-Studies**—Multi-year data syntheses that form the foundation of full accreditation renewal.

In each of these episodes, AI can provide critical decision support. For example, during an annual review, AI-powered dashboards can instantly flag downward trends in field placement performance, prompting early intervention (Salas-Pilco et al., 2022). In mid-cycle evaluations, predictive models can estimate the likelihood of achieving improvement targets under various scenarios (Zawacki-Richter et al., 2019). For targeted improvement plans, NLP tools can rapidly synthesize feedback from multiple stakeholders to inform intervention strategies (Adorni & Ponzini, 2024). These episodes are unique yet interrelated (see Figure 2.1).

Mechanisms for examining these AI-supported episodes will be explored in greater detail in Chapter 5, which describes the direct application of AI tools to designing a quality assurance system that informs continuous improvement.

Automated Data Analysis in Accreditation Reporting

Accreditation bodies require comprehensive evidence: candidate progress data, faculty credentials, curriculum

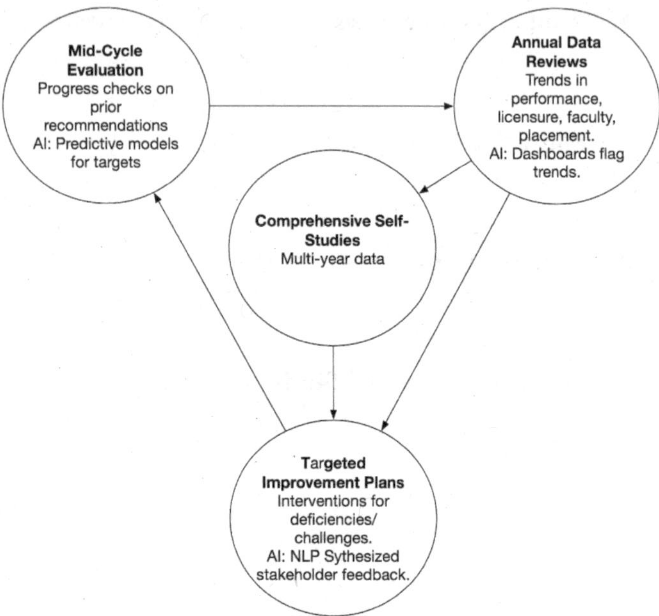

Figure 2.1 Episodes of decision-making with AI.

alignment documents, and field experience records. Traditionally, compiling this evidence has been labor-intensive, often resulting in inconsistencies across reporting cycles (Williamson & Eynon, 2020).

AI transforms this process by:

- Automatically extracting relevant performance indicators from assessment databases
- Using NLP to review narrative reports and identify required evidence (Salas-Pilco et al., 2022)
- Categorizing documentation with machine learning models for rapid retrieval (Stoodley et al., 2024)

The impact is twofold: human error and oversight are minimized, and faculty can devote more energy to interpreting data, engaging in reflective dialogue, and designing responsive interventions (Adorni & Ponzini, 2024; U.S. Department of Education, 2023). By standardizing the evidence-gathering process, AI helps EPPs maintain a state of ongoing readiness for accreditation rather than scrambling to assemble data before deadlines (Holmes et al., 2019).

Predictive Modeling for Candidate and Program Success

Predictive analytics brings a forward-looking dimension to accreditation work (Holmes et al., 2019). By analyzing historical records alongside real-time performance data, AI models can:

- Identify candidates at risk of failing key assessments.
- Predict the potential impact of curriculum changes.
- Anticipate shifts in program outcomes based on resource allocations (Salas-Pilco et al., 2022).

This capability allows EPPs to make early, informed decisions that improve outcomes for both candidates and the program as a whole (Zawacki-Richter et al., 2019). For instance, if predictive analysis suggests that changes in field placement site selection could improve licensure pass rates by 8 percent, leaders can pilot adjustments well before the next accreditation cycle and document the results as evidence of proactive improvement (UNESCO, 2021).

Importantly, these predictions must be handled ethically. Predictive models are only as fair as the data that trains them; if past inequities are embedded in historical data, the predictions may replicate bias (Holmes et al., 2019). This reinforces the need for human oversight and equity-focused review in every predictive application.

Real-Time Analytics for Adaptive Accreditation

The traditional approach to accreditation—annual or biennial reporting—risks basing high-stakes decisions on outdated data. Real-time analytics change that paradigm (U.S. Department of Education, 2023). AI-powered platforms can continuously update dashboards with current performance data, allowing programs to:

- Spot emerging trends as they occur.
- Adjust instructional methods midterm.
- Document and communicate interventions to accrediting bodies in near real time (Salas-Pilco et al., 2022).

This immediacy fosters a culture of responsiveness. For example, if a cohort's performance in a particular assessment dips in the first quarter, faculty can adjust instruction and support measures immediately and track whether those adjustments produce measurable improvements within the same reporting period (Holmes et al., 2019).

Institutional Research and AI-Driven Insight

Institutional research teams are essential partners in accreditation, providing data interpretation and evidence synthesis. AI tools expand their capabilities by integrating multiple datasets into a single analytical environment (Williamson & Eynon, 2020; UNESCO, 2021).

These tools can uncover complex, previously hidden patterns such as the relationship between mentor teacher characteristics and candidate performance in clinical placements (Stoodley et al., 2024). With such insights, programs can refine placement policies, enhance mentoring practices, and strengthen the evidence presented in self-studies (Zawacki-Richter et al., 2019).

Ethics as a Continuous Thread in AI-Supported Accreditation

Ethics cannot be an afterthought in AI use for accreditation. From data privacy to bias prevention, ethical considerations must be embedded in every phase of data-driven decision-making (Holmes et al., 2019). This includes:

- Ensuring data security and confidentiality for sensitive candidate and faculty information.
- Maintaining transparency in how AI models operate and make recommendations (UNESCO, 2021).
- Regularly auditing AI tools for equity and fairness (Holmes et al., 2019).

Weaving ethics into every decision-making episode ensures that accreditation practices remain aligned with professional and societal values. This integration also helps maintain credibility with accrediting bodies, policymakers, and the public (U.S. Department of Education, 2023).

Beyond Continuous Improvement: Strategic Innovation

Continuous improvement is a hallmark of accreditation, but AI offers the opportunity to move into strategic innovation (Williamson & Eynon, 2020; UNESCO, 2021). Scenario modeling allows programs to explore "what-if" conditions:

- What if licensure requirements change within the next two years?
- How would adding more technology-rich field placements affect candidate readiness?
- What adjustments would be needed to meet anticipated standards for AI literacy in teaching?

By running such simulations, programs prepare for possible futures and influence policy by sharing data-informed projections with stakeholders (Holmes et al., 2019; U.S. Department of Education, 2023). This positions the EPP as a thought leader rather than a passive participant in policy changes.

Conclusion

AI is reshaping the accreditation process from a compliance-driven routine into a proactive, strategic enterprise. Through automation, predictive analytics, and real-time monitoring, programs can identify challenges earlier, respond more effectively, and maintain ongoing readiness (Zawacki-Richter et al., 2019; Salas-Pilco et al., 2022). Integrating ethics throughout ensures that these innovations support fairness, transparency, and equity (Holmes et al., 2019; UNESCO, 2021). Moving beyond continuous improvement into strategic innovation allows EPPs to shape the future of teacher preparation, not just adapt to it (Williamson & Eynon, 2020). In Chapter 5, the practical application of these AI tools will be examined in detail, with case examples illustrating how AI can design processes and practice for continuous improvement.

Reflection Points

The following questions are designed to help EPPs critically examine the integration of Artificial Intelligence into accreditation-related data-driven decision-making. These can be used for faculty reflection, accreditation team planning, governance discussions, or professional development workshops.

Ethical Foundations

- How does your institution define *ethical AI use* in accreditation decision-making, and does this definition explicitly address transparency, fairness, and privacy?

- In what ways could current AI-enabled accreditation practices inadvertently compromise ethical principles, and how might they be redesigned to uphold integrity?

- What institutional safeguards are in place to ensure AI tools are used as a complement—not a replacement—for human professional judgment?

Episodes of Decision-Making

- At what points in the accreditation cycle (e.g., evidence collection, data analysis, reporting) could AI most meaningfully enhance decision quality?

- How can your institution ensure that AI-enabled decisions are informed by context-specific knowledge rather than purely statistical outputs?

- What processes could be implemented to document and review AI-supported decisions for accountability and improvement?

Mitigating Bias and Ensuring Equity

- What forms of bias might currently exist in your accreditation data, and how could AI either mitigate or amplify these biases?

- How could bias detection tools be built into accreditation analytics to safeguard against inequitable decisions?
- What metrics could you use to determine whether AI-driven decisions improve equitable outcomes for candidates, faculty, and programs?

Faculty and Stakeholder Engagement

- How might AI adoption shift the role of faculty and staff in crafting your accreditation narrative?
- What strategies could ensure faculty retain control over final interpretations of AI outputs?
- How can students, alumni, and community partners be engaged in the evaluation of AI-assisted accreditation systems?

Governance, Policy, and Transparency

- Does your institution have clear governance structures that define AI's role in accreditation decision-making?
- What transparency measures could be implemented to make AI-supported decisions understandable to accreditors, faculty, and the public?
- How might policy frameworks evolve to address emerging AI capabilities, risks, and compliance requirements?

Continuous Improvement and Strategic Innovation

- How can AI move your accreditation process from periodic, compliance-driven reporting to a real-time, continuous improvement model?

- What scenario-planning exercises could help your institution anticipate and adapt to future accreditation policy changes?

- How might AI be used not just to meet current standards, but to lead innovation in educator preparation quality assurance?

3 Ethical Considerations and Challenges in AI-Driven Teacher Education Accreditation

Introduction

The integration of Artificial Intelligence (AI) in teacher education accreditation presents ethical challenges, warranting focused discussion on its potential benefits and risks. While AI has the potential to streamline accreditation processes, enhance data analysis, and improve decision-making, it also introduces risks related to data privacy, bias, academic integrity, transparency, and faculty autonomy. As educational leaders judiciously integrate AI into the accreditation process, they have an obligation to ensure that this powerful technology is applied in ways that align with professional standards, uphold academic integrity, and advance equity and accountability.

This chapter examines the key ethical considerations related to AI in EPP accreditation, drawing from current peer-reviewed literature and best practices in AI governance.

Data Privacy and Security in AI-Driven Accreditation

As discussed in the previous chapter, one of the foremost ethical concerns in AI implementation is data privacy and security. Accreditation requires collecting vast amounts of data, including student performance metrics, faculty evaluations, and institutional records. As educational leaders leverage AI-driven accreditation tools, they must be mindful to protect the personally identifiable information (PII) of all stakeholders as they comply with regulatory frameworks:

- Family Educational Rights and Privacy Act (FERPA) in the United States;
- General Data Protection Regulation (GDPR) in Europe;
- Institutional Data Governance Policies.

Risks of AI in Accreditation Data Management

Research suggests that as AI models retain and process large datasets, there is an increased risk of data leaks, unauthorized access, and misuse of personal information (Mustapha, 2024). In Chapter 2, we have outlined the power of AI to process large datasets and enhance data analysis to provide data-informed insights. Inherent within the process of leveraging AI to support data-driven decision-making is the need to maintain critical oversight of the protection of stakeholder data. Take into consideration the following risks of AI in data management within the accreditation process:

- AI-driven self-study tools may store sensitive student and faculty data beyond necessary use.

- Cloud-based AI platforms may lack sufficient encryption protocols to protect accreditation records.
- There is the potential for the use of accreditation data by third parties for commercial or unintended purposes.

Ethical Safeguards for Data Protection

Clear guidelines, as demonstrated in Appendix A, help guide decisions, and there are actions we can take to reduce the risk. At the heart of these risks is an obligation by educational leaders to protect sensitive data. Stakeholders' personally identifiable information (PII) is at risk when used as part of the AI-enhanced accreditation processes. To address these risks, institutions should mindfully consider safeguards for protecting sensitive data. The following examples serve as a starting point as institutions develop robust data privacy protocols as part of an AI-enhanced accreditation process:

- Anonymizing all datasets through de-identification techniques (removing personal identifiers from accreditation datasets).
- Ensuring that AI-generated reports are stored in secure institutional repositories.
- Providing clear AI usage policies for faculty and accreditation reviewers (Hoke, 2025), (Appendix A provides one example).
- Seeking verification of data safety and privacy measures within selected AI tools.
- Establishing timelines to delete sensitive data stored as part of the accreditation process.

By implementing ethical AI governance policies, EPPs can balance innovation and privacy compliance in accreditation workflows.

Bias and Equity Concerns in AI Accreditation Models

Bias in AI-driven accreditation is another major ethical challenge. AI models are trained on historical data, which may contain embedded biases related to race, gender, institutional reputation, and socioeconomic factors. These biases can lead to unfair evaluations of educator preparation programs, disproportionately impacting minority-serving institutions, historically Black colleges and universities, and under-resourced programs. This is also a challenge with human systems, as discussed in Chapter 1, subjectivity and inconsistency with human interpretation of complex standards can introduce variability and bias into accreditation judgments as well (Zawacki-Richter et al., 2019).

The Risk of Algorithmic Bias in Accreditation Evaluations

As AI tools become increasingly integrated into education systems and accreditation processes, it is essential to foreground the ethical implications of their use—particularly the risk of algorithmic bias. While AI systems offer unprecedented potential to streamline evaluations, synthesize vast datasets, and surface insights for program improvement, these benefits must be weighed against the risks of replicating and exacerbating existing inequities.

Algorithmic bias occurs when machine learning models or AI systems produce outputs that are systematically prejudiced due to flawed data, model design, or societal context. For example, machine learning models may result in biased and discriminatory outcomes because they replicate patterns in the data used to train them (Ferrara, 2024). These biases may be embedded in the historical data on which systems are trained or may stem from design choices that unintentionally prioritize majority populations. In education, such biases have already been documented in automated essay scoring, emotion detection, and dropout prediction algorithms (Baker & Hawn, 2022).

Algorithmic bias is a structural concern with tangible implications for equity. Bias in AI systems can reinforce and deepen existing societal inequities, resulting in disproportionate harm to marginalized groups and limiting their access to critical resources and opportunities (Ferrara, 2024). Within the context of educator preparation and accreditation, this means that AI systems designed to assess program quality, teacher candidate effectiveness, or institutional outcomes may disadvantage candidates from underrepresented backgrounds if not carefully audited for fairness. The risk is not hypothetical: as AI tools are increasingly deployed in high-stakes evaluation contexts, including CAEP-aligned continuous improvement processes, unexamined bias could compromise both equity and credibility.

In sum, studies have found that bias in AI models can reinforce systemic inequalities in education (Cetin et al., 2024). The following potential risks represent key considerations educational leaders must take as they integrate AI into the accreditation process:

- AI trained on data from elite institutions may disproportionately favor well-resourced programs, thereby disadvantaging smaller, community-based, or minority-serving EPPs.
- When nontraditional, community-driven, or practice-based models are underrepresented in training data, AI systems may undervalue these approaches in accreditation evaluations.

- False positives or inaccurate risk predictions may penalize high-need institutions or those implementing innovative practices.

- Using historical accreditation decisions as training data can perpetuate past evaluation biases, especially those that undervalued culturally responsive or alternative preparation models. AI models may reflect dominant pedagogical norms and institutional practices, marginalizing culturally sustaining or locally relevant approaches to educator preparation.

- AI systems that rely heavily on quantifiable metrics like test scores or employment rates may misrepresent true program quality and ignore structural inequities.

- Predictive tools based on biased historical data may screen out candidates from marginalized backgrounds, reinforcing systemic barriers to entry and success.

- Opaque algorithmic decision-making can erode stakeholder trust, especially when institutions cannot trace or challenge the rationale behind AI-generated judgments.

Strategies to Mitigate Bias

As AI tools are introduced into educational accreditation processes, the potential for algorithmic bias must be addressed with intention and care. Bias has been empirically documented across a range of educational applications—from dropout prediction to essay scoring and emotion detection—demonstrating how systems trained on flawed or incomplete data can produce inequitable outcomes (Baker & Hawn, 2022).

One of the most direct paths to mitigation is improving data quality. When AI systems are trained on datasets that reflect past decisions or structural inequities, those models risk learning and reinforcing historical patterns of exclusion (Agarwal et al., 2023).

In accreditation contexts, this might include prior assumptions about what constitutes "effective" teacher preparation, which may marginalize innovative, community-based, or culturally responsive models.

To reduce this risk, institutions should collect diverse and representative datasets for AI training, ensuring sufficient proportions of all relevant groups and avoiding variables that embed bias (Baker & Hawn, 2022). Without such attention to data composition, AI systems may default to serving the majority population more accurately while misclassifying minority-serving programs (Agarwal et al., 2023).

Human oversight remains essential. Accreditation teams should apply professional judgment to AI-generated reports, using transparency tools that allow them to audit how decisions are made—such as those described by Chu and Sisson (2024)—and to intervene when needed. Regular reviews of subgroup performance are critical to ensure that strong aggregate accuracy does not mask disparities for underrepresented communities (Agarwal et al., 2023).

By committing to representative data, thoughtful oversight, and transparent processes, educational leaders can ensure that AI supports—rather than undermines—the goals of fairness and inclusivity in accreditation.

Academic Integrity and AI's Role in Accreditation Self-Studies

The use of AI in automating self-study reports raises concerns about academic integrity and the authenticity of accreditation documentation. More than a compliance exercise, accreditation is a process of self-evaluation, reflection, and institutional learning that is foundational to continuous improvement. When institutions shortcut this process by overly relying on AI to generate narratives or assemble evidence, they risk diminishing the depth and sincerity of the reflection expected in a robust self-study.

AI should not replace the human insight, professional judgment, and collaborative dialogue that self-studies are designed to cultivate. Instead, AI tools should be leveraged to support and deepen these processes by surfacing patterns in disaggregated data, organizing documentation for review, or prompting institutions to explore trends they may not have otherwise considered. When used appropriately, AI is a technological partner in institutional introspection that can make data more accessible and reflective conversations more grounded. However, its use must be transparent, ethically guided, and centered on empowering—rather than displacing—the professional voices of faculty, staff, and institutional leaders.

The Risk of Overreliance on AI in Self-Studies

AI can accelerate report generation, but institutions must ensure that self-study narratives remain reflective of genuine institutional efforts and faculty perspectives. Ethical risks emerge when AI is used without intentional oversight or meaningful faculty engagement.

While AI can streamline aspects of report writing, its misuse in accreditation self-studies poses several ethical risks. Each of the following highlights the need for transparent protocols, human oversight, and a commitment to preserving the reflective, collaborative nature of the accreditation process.

- AI-generated text may lack the depth, nuance, and contextual understanding that emerge from faculty-led reflection and institutional dialogue.

- Without careful prompting and review, AI tools can produce content that closely resembles previously published self-studies, raising concerns about academic integrity and potential plagiarism (Mustapha, 2024).

- Automating large portions of the self-study may disengage faculty and staff from the reflective processes that accreditation is meant to foster, weakening institutional ownership of findings and recommendations.

- AI systems can generate inaccurate or fabricated information—so-called "hallucinations"—that may misstate institutional data or introduce misleading claims into accreditation documentation.

Ethical Framework for AI in Self-Study Writing

Institutions can maintain academic integrity by:

- Requiring faculty oversight and verification of AI-generated reports.

- Developing AI citation policies to acknowledge the role of AI tools in accreditation documents.

- Using AI as a support tool rather than a replacement for faculty expertise in accreditation decision-making (Voiosu, 2024).

Maintaining a human-centered approach in documentation ensures authenticity and compliance with professional ethics.

A Framework for Iterative AI-Assisted Self-Reporting

As EPPs integrate AI tools into accreditation processes, it is essential to maintain the integrity, authenticity, and reflective depth of self-study reports. The following five-step framework offers an iterative, human-centered approach for ethically incorporating AI into accreditation self-reporting.

1. **Organize Data and Engage in Community Reflection**: Begin by collecting and organizing institutional data aligned with accreditation standards. AI may be used to assist in data cleaning, basic trend identification, or visualization, but faculty and staff must remain central to the interpretation process. Teams should gather to reflect on the meaning behind the data—especially disaggregated results—and discuss implications for equity, program effectiveness, and continuous improvement.

   a. Optional AI use: Ask AI to summarize large datasets or suggest questions for interpreting patterns across sites, cohorts, or demographic groups.

   b. Sample prompt: "Based on this dataset, what disparities in candidate performance might be important for faculty to discuss in relation to Standard 3?"

2. **Assign Prompts and Support Faculty Reflection**: Break into working groups aligned with specific accreditation components (e.g., completer effectiveness, quality assurance systems). Each group engages in written and verbal reflection on how the EPP meets the standard, grounded in evidence and shared professional judgment. This step centers human reflection and avoids premature reliance on AI.

   a. Optional AI use: Request clarifying questions, research citations, or frameworks for deeper thinking.

   b. Sample prompt: "What questions should faculty consider when evaluating how well our program measures completer impact on student learning?"

3. **Use AI for Drafting—Not Defining—Narratives**:
    Once human insights and key ideas are gathered by
    key stakeholders in the accreditation process, AI can
    be prompted to help generate initial narrative drafts.
    However, it is essential that prompts are carefully
    written to avoid AI inserting unsupported claims,
    changing tone, or oversimplifying complex ideas. The
    role of AI here is as a copy editor or drafter, not an
    author.

    a. Sample prompt: "Using the following bulleted
        faculty reflections and data summary, help me
        organize this into a draft response to Standard 4.
        Keep the original language and avoid rewording
        key phrases. Do not make up or add information."

4. **Use AI as a Critical Friend for Iteration and
    Interrogation**: After initial drafts are produced, AI
    can be used to play the role of a critical peer reviewer
    or accreditation coach. Prompt AI to identify gaps,
    challenge assumptions, question unsupported claims,
    and highlight opportunities to deepen reflection.

    a. Sample prompts:
        i.   "What implicit biases or assumptions might be
             present in this draft narrative?"
        ii. "What specific evidence could strengthen this
             section?"
        iii. "Does this response adequately
             address disaggregated data and equity
             considerations?"

5. **Convene for Final Human-Centered Review and
    Editing**: Final narratives should be reviewed and
    edited in community by the leadership team, faculty,
    and relevant stakeholders. This final step is a safeguard
    for academic integrity and an opportunity to align the

voice, tone, and content of the report with institutional values and evidence. AI can support copyediting or consistency checks; the final decisions must rest with humans.

    a. Sample prompt: "Please check this draft for clarity and consistency in tone. Do not add new content or change the meaning of sentences."

Prompting Principles for Ethical AI Use in Accreditation

To support responsible AI integration, EPPs should consider the following guiding principles:

- Be transparent. Clearly document when and how AI tools were used in the drafting process, following institutional AI citation policies.

- Maintain authorship. Ensure that all substantive content originates from faculty, staff, or institutional sources—not the AI itself.

- Review for accuracy. Independently verify any data interpretations, summaries, or claims generated with AI.

- Avoid template thinking. Use AI to organize ideas—not to standardize language in a way that erases institutional voice or context.

Transparency and Explainability in AI Accreditation Systems

Transparency in AI decision-making is crucial for trust and accountability in accreditation. If AI models automatically generate accreditation evaluations without clear explanations, institutions may struggle to challenge inaccurate assessments or understand the rationale behind AI-driven recommendations.

Challenges of AI Opacity in Accreditation

AI models often operate as "black boxes," where the internal decision-making processes are not easily interpretable by faculty or accreditation bodies (Shepherd, 2025). This lack of transparency presents several risks within the context of educator preparation accreditation. For example, an EPP may receive a negative evaluation from an AI-assisted system in the form of a flagged deficiency in candidate outcomes or perceived noncompliance with a specific standard. Educational leaders may find it difficult—or even impossible—to verify how that conclusion was reached, which data were weighted most heavily, or whether the model appropriately accounted for contextual factors such as student demographics, program design, or recent improvement efforts. The inability to explain or trace AI-generated decisions complicates the process of appealing or correcting those judgments, particularly when faculty and administrators lack access to the model's reasoning. Over time, such opacity can erode trust in accreditation outcomes, especially if educators perceive that critical decisions about quality, equity, or compliance are being made by systems they do not understand or cannot interrogate.

Ethical Best Practices for AI Transparency

Ensuring AI transparency in accreditation is a human-centered process that requires proactive leadership, ongoing oversight, and clear communication between institutions and accrediting bodies. Interpretable AI models that provide clear rationales for accreditation evaluations can help build confidence in system outputs. AI-generated decisions should include explicit justifications and evidence sources, enabling educational leaders to assess both the validity and fairness of the conclusions. Accrediting agencies can strengthen trust by establishing review committees that evaluate the transparency, fairness, and contextual appropriateness of AI tools used in accreditation (Tabish, 2024). By embedding explainability and interpretability into AI design and governance, accreditation processes remain accountable, equitable, and open to institutional feedback.

Risks to Faculty Decision-Making

If AI tools gain substantial influence over accreditation reviews, self-study writing, and assessment data analysis, there is a risk that faculty may lose some control over shaping their institution's accreditation narrative. When automated performance evaluations override faculty interpretation, or when AI-driven accreditation models prioritize efficiency at the expense of academic rigor, the result can be a narrowing of perspective. Moreover, faculty expertise may be undervalued if AI-generated reports are afforded more weight than human-authored analysis (Hoke, 2025). These risks underscore the importance of clearly defining how AI is positioned within accreditation processes—not as a decision-maker, but as a support to professional judgment.

Preserving Faculty Autonomy in AI-Driven Accreditation

Upholding academic freedom requires that faculty retain clear authority over AI-assisted accreditation decisions. Institutions should develop governance policies that explicitly define faculty roles in the oversight of AI tools, ensuring that human judgment remains central to the accreditation process. Equally important is positioning AI as a supportive resource rather than a directive force, so that its outputs are used to inform—not dictate—accreditation actions (Cetin et al., 2024). By embedding these safeguards, institutions can balance the efficiency gains of AI with the scholarly rigor and contextual insight that only faculty bring.

Conclusion

In conclusion, the adoption of AI in social sciences education presents both unprecedented opportunities and complex challenges. Successfully navigating this transformative era demands more than technological implementation—it requires strategic vision, robust ethical governance, and inclusive collaboration among educators, policymakers, and technologists. By prioritizing digital literacy, fostering critical thinking, and ensuring equitable access, institutions can harness AI's potential to not only enhance learning outcomes but also to shape a more informed, innovative, and socially responsible generation of scholars.

Within teacher education accreditation, the integration of AI offers transformative potential to improve quality and efficiency, but it also brings significant ethical challenges such as data privacy, bias mitigation, academic integrity, transparency, and faculty autonomy. To ensure that AI supports rather than undermines accreditation processes, institutions must adopt ethical AI frameworks, maintain human oversight, and implement transparent governance policies. By proactively addressing these ethical concerns, AI can serve as a powerful force to enhance the quality, fairness, and accountability of educator preparation program accreditation. Looking ahead, sustained research, cross-sector collaboration, and adaptive policy development will be essential to fully realize AI's benefits while safeguarding the integrity of educational systems worldwide.

Reflection Points

The following questions are designed to help educator preparation programs critically engage with the ethical, practical, and strategic considerations of integrating Artificial Intelligence into accreditation processes. These questions may be used for individual reflection, team discussions, or as part of institutional planning and professional development activities.

Ethical Foundations

- How does your institution currently define "ethical AI use" in accreditation contexts, and how might that definition need to evolve?

- Where does your program's current use of technology fall short of meeting high standards of professional, pedagogical, and andragogical practice?

- What processes ensure that AI applications align with academic integrity, equity, and accountability?

Mitigating Bias

- In your current accreditation processes, what types of bias—if any—might already exist in the data you collect?

- How could you assess whether your accreditation data represents all relevant groups equitably?

- What would it take to integrate regular bias audits into your AI-driven accreditation systems?

Faculty Decision-Making

- How might AI adoption impact the way faculty shape the accreditation narrative at your institution?

- What safeguards could be implemented to ensure faculty judgment remains the final authority in accreditation decisions?

- How can AI be positioned as a cognitive partner rather than a substitute for faculty expertise?

Human-Centered AI Integration

- What steps could your program take to design AI tools that reflect the values, priorities, and lived experiences of your faculty and students?

- How could faculty and staff be more actively involved in the development, training, and evaluation of AI tools used in accreditation?

- What training or professional development would help faculty confidently interpret and challenge AI outputs?

Governance, Policy, and Transparency

- Does your institution currently have policies that govern AI use in accreditation or related decision-making? If not, where would you start?

- How might transparency and explainability be built into any AI tool used for accreditation purposes?

- What accountability mechanisms would reassure faculty, students, and the public that AI tools are serving the institution's mission?

Continuous Improvement and Equity

- How could AI be embedded into your accreditation process to create a *continuous* rather than episodic cycle of improvement?

- What indicators would you monitor to ensure that AI-supported accreditation processes advance equity rather than replicate historical inequities?

- How could you evaluate whether AI is helping—not hindering—your institution's long-term improvement goals?

4 AI in Self-Study Reports and Accreditation Compliance

Introduction

AI is reshaping higher education in terms of instructional design and student learning, as well as in the behind-the-scenes work of accreditation and continuous improvement. One of the most resource-intensive elements of accreditation is the self-study report: a comprehensive narrative aligned with standards that outlines evidence, describes institutional processes, and demonstrates impact. This chapter explores how AI tools enhance the creation, organization, and analysis of self-study reports, improve alignment with accreditation requirements such as CAEP and state standards, and help institutions maintain ongoing compliance with reduced faculty burden.

As institutions face increasing expectations for transparency, equity, and data-informed decision-making, AI offers a new set of tools to meet these demands efficiently. By leveraging machine learning, natural language processing, and smart document management systems, EPPs can improve documentation, streamline workflows, and better prepare for both internal and external review. These changes reflect broader shifts in educational technology policy and research, including the US Department of Education's recent report emphasizing AI's potential to support continuous improvement and instructional quality (Office of Educational Technology, 2023). The insights and tools discussed in this chapter are grounded in current research and practice, including findings by Zawacki-Richter et al. (2019), Alexandrowicz (2024), Baidoo-Anu and Owusu Ansah (2023), and broader analyses of AI's challenges and opportunities in higher education (Akinwalere & Ivanov, 2022).

AI-Enhanced Self-Study Report Writing

The process of writing self-study reports has traditionally relied on extensive collaboration across departments, requiring faculty and staff to synthesize data, narratives, and evidence into coherent documents aligned with standards. This can take months or even years of planning. With recent advances in natural language processing (NLP), AI-powered writing assistants—such as OpenAI's ChatGPT, Jasper, and other large language models (LLMs)—are increasingly being used to generate initial narrative drafts, summarize findings, and support language refinement.

When trained on past accreditation documents or fed institution-specific prompts, these models can generate structured narratives that reflect the tone and terminology expected in accreditation contexts. For example, a prompt such as "Generate a response to CAEP Standard R5.2 emphasizing data reliability and stakeholder engagement" can yield a well-organized paragraph that faculty can refine. LLMs also function as "thought partners," supporting faculty in examining multiple interpretations of data and crafting narratives that better represent institutional nuance.

Moreover, Alexandrowicz (2024) emphasizes that AI integration in teacher education not only enhances administrative tasks but also fosters transformative pedagogy by encouraging reflective practice among educators. This suggests that AI-supported self-study processes can promote deeper faculty engagement with accreditation standards, moving beyond compliance to pedagogical transformation.

While AI tools cannot replace the deep contextual knowledge of faculty, they can significantly reduce the burden of the initial drafting process. They assist in maintaining consistency in voice and alignment across standards and allow faculty to focus their attention on verifying claims, interpreting data, and ensuring narratives are reflective of actual practices. As Singleton (2025) reports, institutions that pilot AI tools in report writing have noted improvements in both efficiency and the clarity of their reports.

These practices align with broader developments in learning analytics and educational data mining. Bienkowski, Feng, and Means (2012) argue that technologies that assist in interpreting educational data play a critical role in enhancing teaching and institutional effectiveness. As AI becomes more embedded in quality assurance workflows, its value in framing data for storytelling and compliance will continue to grow.

While these tools reduce drafting time, they are not infallible. Faculty must review outputs for nuance, validate claims, and ensure alignment with authentic institutional experiences. AI-supported drafting is already improving the consistency and accessibility of accreditation documentation. This trend parallels learning analytics and educational data mining, which have long supported data-informed narrative development (Bienkowski et al., 2012; Sclater, 2017). As AI evolves, these capabilities are becoming increasingly actionable at the program and institutional levels.

As we have demonstrated, AI provides many affordances, while also requiring guard rails (see Figure 4.1). While AI-powered drafting accelerates the creation of narratives, accreditation also depends on clear evidence alignment. The next step is mapping

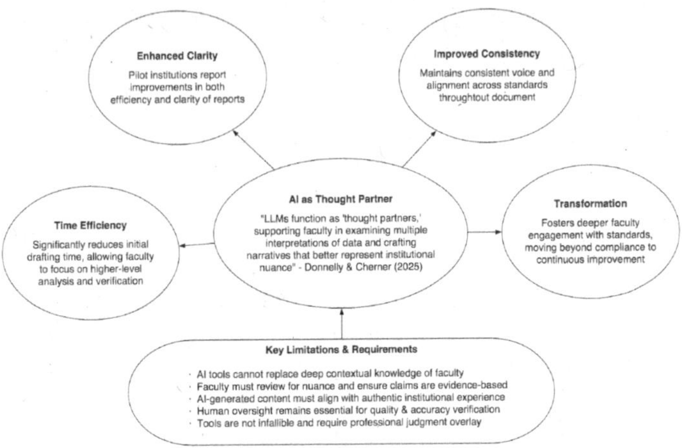

Figure 4.1 Advantages and limitations of AI in self-study report writing.

artifacts to the correct standards—a process that AI can now streamline dramatically.

Mapping Accreditation Evidence to Standards Using AI Algorithms

Beyond writing narratives, a major challenge lies in aligning large volumes of evidence to the correct accreditation standards. AI algorithms can assist in tagging, sorting, and mapping documents to both national (e.g., CAEP) and state-level standards through supervised machine learning and semantic search capabilities.

Smart document repositories, such as those built on platforms like Accreditation Intelligence and Reporting Tools, use trained models to classify artifacts based on language patterns, file metadata, and contextual keywords. For example, lesson plans with embedded formative assessments might be automatically linked to CAEP R1.2 or InTASC Standard 6. These tools can also create visual matrices or dashboards showing where evidence is strong, duplicated, or missing—giving faculty real-time feedback to address gaps proactively. This significantly reduces the manual labor of cross-referencing and ensures a more comprehensive mapping process. These mapping capabilities also reflect deeper transformations in how institutions manage quality. Cayirtepe and Cizmeci Senel (2022) suggest that AI-enhanced self-assessment systems can increase standardization in quality assurance reporting, particularly when tied to decision-support systems that reduce manual subjectivity. Accuracy, however, remains a concern. Zawacki-Richter et al. (2019) highlight that many AI systems in higher education are developed without sufficient educator involvement, which may result in tools that are efficient but disconnected from pedagogical or institutional realities. Faculty participation in AI design and training remains essential to ensure the tools meet accreditation expectations without compromising educational integrity.

Once evidence is accurately mapped to Standards, AI can further enhance accreditation readiness by reducing the workload associated with ongoing compliance tasks.

AI for Faculty Workload Reduction and Institutional Compliance

One of the most significant impacts of AI in accreditation is its ability to reduce repetitive tasks and allow faculty to focus on high-impact activities. In the context of self-studies and ongoing compliance, AI can be deployed to automate routine documentation tasks such as summarizing meeting notes, tracking course changes, or generating annual program reports.

When integrated into institutional Quality Assurance Systems (QAS), AI can also flag missing documentation, identify outdated evidence, and prompt departments to upload required materials before deadlines. Predictive tools may suggest likely areas of noncompliance based on past data trends or accreditation outcomes, allowing for timely interventions.

AI-powered communication tools can significantly reduce faculty overload by summarizing accreditation-related documents, distributing tasks, and even generating real-time updates aligned with evolving policy frameworks. These systems function as expert assistants, as seen in various studies on AI applications in higher education administration and evaluation (Ifenthaler & Yau, 2020; Renz & Hilbig, 2020; Zawacki-Richter et al., 2019).

Institutions adopting these tools report higher faculty morale, improved clarity in compliance tasks, and faster report cycles. Still, ethical considerations must be addressed. Overreliance on automation could lead to shallow compliance if critical reflection and professional judgment are overlooked. AI must be used to support, not replace, the human element of educational quality assurance. These tools complement what the US Department of Education (2023) identifies as critical to the future of teaching and learning: ensuring that AI enhances human capacity rather than undermines professional roles. In addition to supporting preparation, AI is increasingly being used to simulate accreditation review processes themselves. Internal audits powered by AI can replicate reviewer logic to identify inconsistencies, gaps in evidence, or misaligned narratives. Some systems generate preliminary feedback reports, highlight contradictory statements, or score alignment with standards based on past rubric models. Chatbot-style assistants are also emerging, allowing faculty or review teams to ask questions like, "Of my current evidence, which ones align to CAEP Standard R5.3?" and receive AI-generated links to documents, summaries, or narrative excerpts. Advanced tools integrate directly with digital accreditation platforms (e.g., Watermark, HelioCampus), allowing seamless updates and version control. Dashboards provide institutional leaders with real-time snapshots of accreditation progress, risk areas, and document currency, replacing static spreadsheets with dynamic, interactive systems. Shifts in how institutions engage with accreditation, especially through AI, are also reshaping curriculum design, as programs move to more agile, compliance-informed structures. These changes reflect a growing convergence between operational systems and academic planning, with implications for long-term curricular innovation.

AI might also support organizational reflection and evaluation efforts when prompted to be a critical thought partner. Rather than only cataloging evidence, AI can be leveraged to pose probing questions, surface overlooked patterns, and generate alternative interpretations of institutional data. For example, natural language models can highlight where self-study narratives emphasize compliance over authentic improvement, or where student outcome data suggests hidden inequities across subgroups. By positioning AI as a mirror, rather than merely a monitor, institutions can foster deeper cycles of inquiry aligned with continuous improvement. The self-study process is not simply about demonstrating compliance; this critical component of accreditation enables EPPs to cultivate a culture of evidence-based reflection and forward planning. In this way, AI becomes a catalyst for more robust organizational learning, encouraging faculty and leaders to interrogate assumptions and identify opportunities for sustainable growth. While automation can streamline the audit cycle and enhance transparency, AI-driven reviews must be rigorously validated to ensure fairness and interpretability. Review decisions should always involve human confirmation, particularly in high-stakes accreditation determinations. AI can prepare the institution, but accountability must remain with the humans behind the systems. Use of these tools is not without risks. As Sclater (2017) explains, the interpretability and fairness of algorithmic outputs must be carefully managed, especially when AI-generated summaries or scores influence high-stakes outcomes. Accreditation, at its core, involves judgment and that judgment must be grounded in human expertise.

Caveats for Using AI in Report Generation

Using AI to create accreditation reports can be a powerful tool, but it comes with significant caveats that reviewers and institutions must keep in mind. One of the primary risks is that AI-generated text can appear convincing at face value. Because AI models are designed to produce coherent, authoritative-sounding prose, the resulting reports may look polished and credible even when they contain inaccuracies or misleading claims. This can create a false sense of confidence in the document, where readers accept content without scrutinizing whether the evidence and reasoning actually support accreditation requirements.

Accreditation standards often require nuanced judgments about evidence, context, and alignment with criteria. AI systems are not capable of true understanding; they generate responses based on patterns in training data. As a result, they may misinterpret institutional data, overlook context-specific details, or apply generic language inappropriately. What looks like a well-argued narrative may in fact miss the nuance that human reviewers would recognize as essential to making a valid case.

Additionally, AI will almost always "provide something," but the output may not be valid or accurate. This is especially problematic when writer intent matters; accreditation reports demonstrate intentionality, reflection, and continuous improvement. AI cannot substitute for institutional voice or purpose. If used whole cloth, the report may sound correct but fail to reflect the genuine practices, values, or progress of the program under review. An EPP must be able to defend the report and have documentation and evidence to support claims. Equally as important as documentation is the ability of faculty, staff, and stakeholders to be able to understand, communicate, and implement the processes described in reports.

If AI is used to construct the narrative and connections of data and process, but those connections do not reflect the institution's actual practices or the analysis and triangulation are inaccurate, the resulting report becomes misleading. Accreditation is fundamentally about demonstrating fidelity between what an institution claims and what it actually does. When the narrative is artificially generated without grounding in lived practice, the risk is that the report showcases an idealized version of compliance rather than authentic evidence of quality assurance. If faculty and staff cannot explain or answer questions regarding reporting, this disconnect can erode the credibility of the institution and raise questions about the integrity of the presented materials. Moreover, inaccurate data analysis undermines the very purpose of accreditation, which relies on valid evidence to assess effectiveness. AI may suggest patterns, relationships, or triangulations that look plausible but have no basis in actual data. Such false linkages can create a surface-level impression of rigor while hiding weaknesses in assessments or performance. Instead of demonstrating reflective practice and continuous improvement, the report may present a distorted picture that fails to support meaningful accountability.

This misuse of AI also strips away the critical element of institutional intent and reflection. Accreditation narratives are not just compliance documents; they are opportunities for programs to analyze their work, acknowledge challenges, and articulate strategies for growth. If AI produces the narrative without the authentic engagement of faculty, staff, and leadership, the institution loses the opportunity for collective learning and improvement. In this sense, AI-generated but inaccurate reports not only risk rejection by accrediting bodies but also short-circuit the internal improvement processes that accreditation is meant to foster.

To guard against these risks, faculty and institutional leaders must be the primary authors of ideas, patterns, and interpretations. Human expertise should drive the initial articulation of findings, outlining how evidence connects to standards and where gaps or opportunities for growth exist. Once this intellectual groundwork is established, AI can be used to refine the prose, linking ideas together, ensuring consistency in voice, or highlighting where additional evidence might be needed. AI serves as a writing partner that enhances clarity and cohesion without displacing the intentional reflection that only humans can provide. This sequencing preserves the authenticity of institutional voice while still leveraging AI's strengths in organization and drafting. It also ensures that the final product is polished and defensible because it reflects the lived practices and insights of the people most intimately engaged in the work.

Finally, AI systems sometimes produce ghost references and incorrect connections—citations or source attributions that look plausible but do not actually exist, or logical links between ideas that are overstated or unfounded. Anytime you use AI this will happen. At the preliminary stages of gathering references for this book, several AI-generated citations appeared legitimate but, upon closer inspection, could not be located in any database. While AI can be a time-saver, its outputs must always undergo human review and verification. This safeguard should be standard practice. In an accreditation context, this is especially dangerous because credibility depends on transparent, verifiable evidence. A report peppered with false connections or analysis could undermine trust not only in the report itself but also in the institution's integrity. Once reviewers detect even a few problematic examples or data analysis disconnects, the entire process may come under suspicion.

This can lead to prolonged interviews or verifications to clarify processes and findings. This creates reputational risks that extend beyond the accreditation cycle, potentially damaging the institution's relationship with its accreditor, partners, and candidates.

Future Directions

Looking ahead, emerging AI tools may further transform accreditation by enabling predictive analytics for site visits, adaptive compliance dashboards, and continuous feedback loops between faculty, students, and accrediting bodies. As these technologies advance, educator preparation programs will need to remain agile, balancing innovation with the core human judgment that provided the structure of educational quality. Users need to view AI as a tool rather than a replacement for human critical thinking. Overreliance on automation will lead to shallow compliance if critical reflection is overlooked. AI must be used to support not replace the human element of educational quality assurance.

Conclusion

AI is rapidly becoming an indispensable ally in the accreditation process, particularly for educator preparation programs facing increased documentation demands, equity reporting requirements, and multi-level compliance expectations. From drafting self-study narratives to mapping evidence and simulating review processes, AI tools have the potential to improve efficiency, reduce workload, and enhance institutional readiness. This requires not only access to technology but also culturally responsive pedagogical integration to ensure AI benefits are equitably distributed.

However, as with all technological innovations, these benefits must be balanced with ethical oversight, contextual understanding, and active faculty engagement. Rather than automating compliance for its own sake, institutions should use AI to create space for reflection, improvement, and deeper conversations about educational quality and equity.

As Zawacki-Richter et al. (2019) remind us, AI in higher education must involve—not replace—educators. Accreditation is, at its core, a human-centered process. While AI can accelerate evidence gathering, narrative drafting, and standards alignment, it cannot replace the professional judgment, contextual expertise, and shared governance that give meaning to accreditation outcomes. The most promising future lies in a hybrid model—one where AI amplifies human capacity, ensures equitable access to quality assurance tools, and supports the continuous pursuit of excellence in teaching and learning.

Reflection Points

The following questions are designed to help educator preparation programs consider how Artificial Intelligence can enhance, streamline, and safeguard the processes of self-study report creation, evidence mapping, and accreditation compliance. These questions can guide individual reflection, facilitate collaborative dialogue, and support strategic planning for responsible AI integration.

AI-Supported Self-Study Narratives

- Which portions of your current self-study report process are most time-consuming or prone to duplication of effort?

- How might AI-powered drafting tools help maintain consistency in tone, structure, and terminology across multiple standards?

- What safeguards will you put in place to ensure that AI-generated narratives accurately reflect institutional realities?

Evidence Mapping and Alignment

- In what ways could AI-assisted mapping tools improve your ability to align artifacts with CAEP, InTASC, or state standards?

- How might real-time dashboards or gap analyses influence your approach to evidence collection?

- What risks might arise if AI misclassifies or overlooks important documentation, and how would you mitigate them?

Reducing Faculty Burden While Maintaining Engagement

- Which accreditation-related tasks could AI automate without diminishing faculty's critical role in analysis and decision-making?

- How could AI free up faculty time for higher-order activities such as strategic planning and curriculum design?

- What professional development would be needed to help faculty use AI tools effectively and ethically?

Ethical Oversight and Quality Assurance

- How will you ensure transparency in how AI selects, tags, or drafts accreditation materials?

- What processes will you implement to validate AI outputs before they are included in official reports?

- How might you balance efficiency gains with the need for deep, human-centered review?

Looking Forward

- Which AI capabilities discussed in this chapter are most applicable to your institution's current accreditation challenges?

- How might piloting AI tools in a limited scope (e.g., one standard or domain) inform broader adoption?

- What measures will you take to ensure that AI integration enhances—not erodes—your institution's culture of continuous improvement?

5 Creating a Quality Assurance System (QAS) for Continuous Improvement and Efficiency

Introduction

Continuous improvement is a cornerstone of accreditation, but its sustainability often depends on the strength of a program's Quality Assurance System (QAS). A well-designed QAS balances structural elements—such as policies, processes, and data systems—with cultural elements that foster faculty engagement, shared ownership, and a commitment to equity. This chapter focuses on the strategic frameworks and guiding principles for designing such systems, highlighting how AI can support alignment, efficiency, and ethical practice. To maintain clarity, the chapter emphasizes big-picture models and decision points, while the more detailed examples—such as data matrices, rubric outputs, and procedural flowcharts—are available on the book website for readers seeking technical demonstrations. In this way, the chapter provides a conceptual foundation, while the appendix B (Bloomsbury.pub/leveragingai) offers applied illustrations to adapt in practice. In this chapter, we begin by discussing the theoretical foundations of Quality Assessment Systems (QAS). We then describe how Artificial Intelligence (AI) could be adopted to enhance and inform these systems (Section 1). Following that, we will examine the ethical considerations associated with this adoption (Section 2). Finally, available on the book website, we present a practical example that illustrates how we utilized AI to design a QAS. This example is not intended as a definitive blueprint, but rather to demonstrate starting points that others can develop and adapt in a short period, laying the groundwork for an adaptive, sustainable QAS capable of driving ongoing, effective improvement.

Framework

The literature on QAS consistently emphasizes the need to strike a balance between structural systems and cultural engagement. This balance is crucial for the success of a QAS, as it ensures that the "hard" dimensions of quality assurance (policies, resources, systems) are complemented by the "soft" dimensions (shared values, ownership, faculty and stakeholder participation), thereby fostering a culture of quality.

The systematic review of the literature conducted by Krooi et al. resulted in a 3P model for framing essential components of "quality" QASs: purposes, processes, and people (2024). QAS must include clear objectives (purposes), efficient methods (processes), and active involvement of all stakeholders (people). These must be aligned for a fully functional system. AI can play a valuable role on the structural side by mapping multiple standards, priorities, and inputs, integrating diverse data sources, and supporting continuous monitoring to support alignment. The importance of faculty and staff engagement, as highlighted by Bendermacher et al. (2017), stresses the need to incorporate voice into any AI application, as well as being essential for monitoring accuracy and the ethical considerations of the processes.

These comprehensive literature review studies inspire a dual approach to QAS design: first, we leverage AI to enhance structural efficiency, data integration, and continuous improvement, as introduced in Chapter 4. This use of AI provides a robust and effective system that can be trusted to deliver results. Second, we embed these tools within a quality culture that fosters faculty engagement, shared ownership, and ethical responsibility, ensuring a balanced and ethical approach to QAS design.

What do QAS need to include? QAS's purpose informs its design and implementation, while intentional attention to the people involved proves critical for success. Section 1 focuses on the integration of Artificial Intelligence (AI) to enhance and inform these quality assurance systems, including a description of the steps we propose for using AI as a tool for creating a QAS. Step 1 demonstrates the use of AI to design a QAS structure, while Step 2 utilizes AI to help identify and synthesize data that comprises the system. We then shift our focus to the processes. Step 3 discusses the use of AI to help create policies for utilizing and maintaining the QAS. Step 4 outlines procedures for implementing policies and promoting continuous improvement, with a focus on the individuals involved in the processes. Section 2 discusses the ethical considerations, including the responsibilities of and for the people involved with the QAS, those who use the QAS, and the subject of the QAS. Sections 1 and 2 encompass the 3P model (QAS alignment of purposes, processes, and people), as discussed above by Krooi et al. (2024). Appendix B (Bloomsbury.pub/leveragingai) provides an example of an outcome achieved through the application of these steps. A quality QAS can help address two concerns from Chapter 1, fragmented data systems (disparate databases and software platforms impede comprehensive, integrated analysis) (Zawacki-Richter et al., 2019) and delayed feedback loops: traditional accreditation cycles produce static reports, hindering timely interventions (Mhlanga, 2023).

Section 1: Creating a Quality QAS

We begin our discussion around the structure and resources. What needs to be included in the QAS? We choose to adapt the backward design model presented by Wiggins and McTighe (2005), which involves first identifying the desired results, determining the acceptable evidence, and planning the process and procedures for implementation. Note: in this context, "acceptable evidence" refers to the means by which we determine that the implementation of procedures and processes has resulted in the desired outcome. We began by asking ChatGPT, an AI language model, the following prompt: "Use backward design to design a quality assurance system for an educator preparation program." The result is represented in Figure 5.1 (OpenAI, 2025).

This figure represents the initial design of the QAS using the backward design model. It provides a visual representation of the key components and their relationships. The process begins with identifying desired results, including compliance with accreditation standards, demonstrating program effectiveness, and cultivating a culture of continuous improvement that engages faculty, candidates, completers, and P–12 partners. Evidence to support these goals is then determined through clearly defined data sources, performance benchmarks, and indicators of system effectiveness, ensuring alignment between standards and program needs. Finally, processes and learning experiences are planned by building strong systems for data collection and management, establishing review cycles, and embedding shared governance in decision-making. Closing the loop is emphasized through written action plans with measurable goals and accountability, while faculty development in data literacy further supports a culture of improvement. This outcome ensures that the QAS both demonstrates compliance and also drives meaningful program growth and innovation;

Identify Desired Results	

Compliance and Accreditation
  - Data needed to demonstrate meeting standard
  - System designed that meets standards
Program Effectiveness
  - Data used to monitor candidates' progression.
  - Data used to used to inform program goals
Continuous Improvement Culture
    Engages faculty, P-12 partners, candidates and
    completers in reviewing data and making
    program changes
Other?	

Determine Acceptable Evidence		
Data Sources What data do we need to show we are meeting the standards and inform our program?	**Performance Benchmarks** Clearly defined performance expectations. Established thresholds for program quality metrics.	**System Effectiveness** Indicators of effectiveness and regular review cycles.

Plan Learning Experiences and Processes	
Data Collection & Management: Build/adapt a data dashboard. Assign ownership for data entry, cleaning and analysis. **Data Review Cycle:** Define **Governance & Decision-Making:** QAS Committee with faculty, P-12 partners, candidates, and staff.	**Closing the Loop:** Written action plans with timelines, responsible parties, and measurable success **Continuous Improvement Culture:** Faculty development on data literacy and analysis

Figure 5.1 Backward design applied to QAS. Adapted from Wiggins and McTighe (2005).

however, the level of detail was insufficient to inform specific actions. We propose the following four steps to unpack this design.

Step 1: Creating the Framework for the QAS

The reporting bodies and purpose of the QAS create the "prompt" for the AI system. The prompt requires specific information to inform the structure and particular resources/data. In this context, the obvious starting points are accreditation standards' requirements and state and federal requirements.

However, limiting the QAS to these two spaces perpetuates the misconception that QASs are solely for compliance, rather than also serving as the linchpin for continuous improvement. To take advantage of the opportunity to truly inform programs based not only on state and national standards but also on the priorities, mission, vision, and goals of the institution and community, it is critical to include faculty and stakeholders in identifying priorities. Finally, colleges and universities often have additional reporting and requirements in place for decision-making in QASs. Incorporating these needs into the design builds efficiencies into the model that can also inform decision-makers (Figure 5.2).

Including all these constituents' voices and input can be labor-intensive, and by the time it is completed, it often requires reevaluation. AI provides an efficient way to synthesize across multiple, sometimes competing, interests to inform the intended desired result from the QAS quickly. This process can result in a list of targeted outcomes and data sources for a

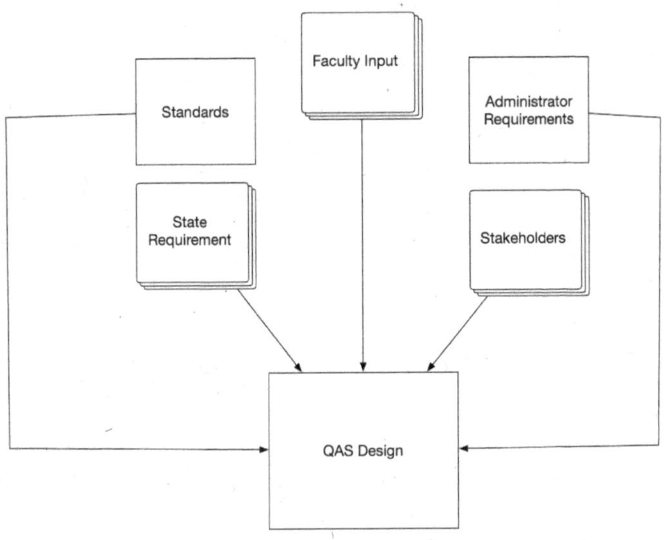

Figure 5.2 Designing quality assurance systems.

system, and ultimately provide a matrix aligning each with the areas that inform the prompt (such as accrediting standards, state standards, local priorities, etc.). Stakeholders, internal and external, then evaluate the results and provide feedback to adapt as needed.

Step 2: Data for the QAS

A matrix of the components aligned with the input discussed above identifies data sources broadly that can inform the various reporting requirements. The next step is to identify the specific data that need to be collected and processed. Prompting AI again results in a list of sources of evidence to address the desired outcomes identified in the matrix. Note that data includes both raw data collected and processed data that will inform continuous improvement (see Figure 5.3).

Part of the QAS analyzes data to inform reporting and continuous improvement. The results of the analyses become "processed data" for later syntheses. In Chapter 2, we unpacked

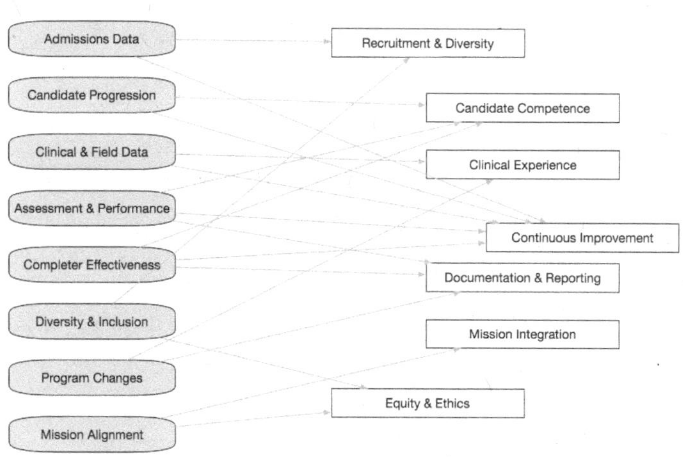

Figure 5.3 Flow of raw data inputs into QAS outcomes.

various methods for processing data in the QAS. In this section, for continuous improvement, determining the processed data for review becomes critical. Processed data can be used for standard analysis reporting. For example, programs might look at disaggregated state test results for their program annually. These processed data reports would be routinely created and part of the QAS data repository, externally sourced, and may not require AI intervention at this stage.

Deciding on specific data depends on the task. AI can recommend data for a dashboard to support routine, annual, or recurring tasks, but the ultimate decision remains with the user. What annually processed data might be helpful for program review? Title II reporting? Accreditation annual report?

Data provided to the system must be both valid and reliable. Unit-created assessments must undergo rigorous evaluations of validity and reliability of the data. This, too, provides a space where AI can inform the work. Garbage in, garbage out is true with humans and AI analysis. Artificial Intelligence can strengthen the validity and reliability of instruments used to measure student learning by supporting both the design and evaluation of assessments. For validity, AI can analyze assessment items against learning objectives, standards, and course outcomes to ensure alignment between what is measured and the intended constructs. It can also assist faculty in writing high-quality rubrics by suggesting performance descriptors, consistently leveling criteria across categories, and checking for clarity and bias in language. However, depending on AI creation of rubrics in and of itself a stamp of reliability is problematic. Fernández-Sánchez et al. identified that people who supplied AI with clear activities, curricular elements, and well-defined objectives produced stronger, more balanced rubrics that aligned closely with curricular goals. High-quality, detailed inputs improved rubric consistency and comprehensiveness. However, the effectiveness of the AI-generated rubrics still depended heavily on the quality of the objectives provided. When people offered vague or poorly formulated objectives, the AI simply added more items without improving quality, sometimes weakening the final rubric. AI can assist in creating reliable tools, but determination of reliability still requires expertise of the user (2025). Care for the creation of the rubrics and expert interrogation are still necessary (Kahlow, 2024). "AI created" is not a sufficient argument for validity since AI is often unable to identify nuance or context-specific components. Concurrent and predictive validity align with the AI protocol; whereas, construct validity requires attention to surrounding details, thus dependent on the human/AI interaction (Azzam, 2023). For reliability, AI tools can detect inconsistencies in rubric application by comparing human scoring patterns with automated scoring models. AI can also support inter-rater consistency by comparing scoring patterns across evaluators, identifying discrepancies, and suggesting calibration sessions when drift is detected. In addition, AI can simulate large-scale test administrations to generate stability estimates and item analysis reports, such as difficulty and discrimination indices, although this might be less likely to be used in this context. When used in partnership with human expertise, AI provides scalable and efficient ways to refine rubrics and assessments so they remain accurate, equitable, and trustworthy measures of student learning.

The system also needs to be prepared for the idiosyncratic questions that arise, where the raw data could inform, but as provided, would be challenging to interpret and incomplete. AI could facilitate this stage of analysis, not only providing data analysis support but also completing a gap analysis to help identify areas where additional data might be necessary to collect. This analysis can then inform decisions about whether to update the QAS or if it is a one-time analysis.

Step 3: Policies

To this point, we have discussed the processes for identifying, storing, and processing data. We have demonstrated the power of AI in assisting with identifying what data to collect and pinpointing gaps. Staff can harvest, analyze, and maintain this system. The critical next steps involve using the data to answer programmatic questions. How will the system be used and maintained? Figure 5.4 identifies topics for consideration for the purpose of policies. The following expands on these topics. This is not intended to be a conclusive list, but provides a snapshot of possibilities.

- Governance and Oversight
  - Establish a Quality Assurance Council with faculty, staff, administrators, and P–12 partners.

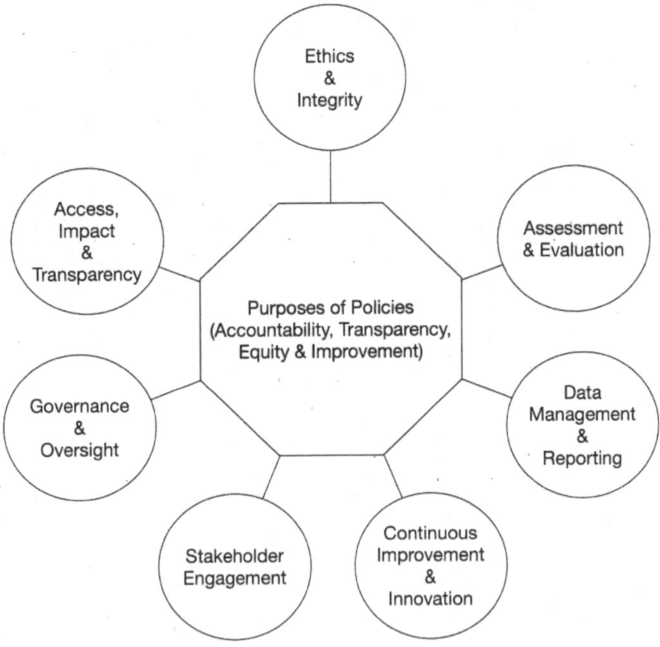

Figure 5.4 Purpose of policies for QAS systems and AI.

- Define decision-making authority and accountability pathways within the unit.
  - Ensure alignment with university-level QAS policies, accreditation, and state and federal requirements.
- Data Management and Reporting
  - Create a Data Governance Policy that sets standards for the collection, retention, and dissemination of data.
  - Ensure compliance with Title II, state reporting, HLC program review, and accreditation standards.
  - Maintain a centralized Data Warehouse accessible to program coordinators.
- Assessment and Evaluation
  - Require validity and reliability checks for all course-embedded and program-level assessments used for evaluation.
  - Define expectations for rubrics, scoring calibration, and evidence documentation across programs.
  - Institute annual faculty reviews of assessment data to "close the loop."
- Continuous Improvement and Innovation
  - Mandate annual program self-studies with analysis of key performance indicators.
  - Require programs to document improvements made and tested.
  - Build a policy for piloting and scaling innovative practices (AI analytics, recruitment models, clinical tools).
- Stakeholder Engagement
  - Require advisory boards for all initial and advanced programs, including those serving P–12 and community representatives.

- Establish formal mechanisms for student, alums, and employer feedback.
  - Ensure partnership policies for school districts are consistently applied and reviewed.
- Access, Impact, and Transparency
  - Develop a fairness audit policy that requires annual review of enrollment, retention, and licensure outcomes by demographic group.
  - Publish annual dashboards on candidate success, employment, and impact on P–12 learning.
  - Align with the unit's mission and faculty belief statements on access and fairness.
- Ethics and Integrity
  - Adopt a Code of Assessment Ethics, including rules on data privacy, faculty responsibility, and candidate fairness.
  - Establish safeguards against misuse of AI, predictive analytics, or assessment results.
  - Require training for faculty and staff in responsible data use and decision-making (Informed by ChatGPT [OpenAI, 2025]).

Each of the topics above provides areas where policies could be developed and documented within the system. Aligning these with the identified themes in Step 1 creates an internally consistent system.

AI can be a powerful partner in both creating and implementing these policies within a unit's Quality Assurance System (QAS). During policy development, AI can analyze large amounts of accreditation standards, state and federal regulations, and professional frameworks using natural language processing (NLP), helping to identify overlaps and gaps and ensuring that all voices are included. AI can contribute to the implementation of established policies by automating processes for timely information gathering while attending to validation and reliability checks. AI-informed analysis can also reveal disparities in candidate outcomes, providing actionable evidence to inform the improvement of fairness policies. AI can verify the validity and reliability of course-embedded measures, supporting best evaluation practices for quality assessments. Continuous improvement over time requires attention to trends, which AI can monitor. At the same time, AI can enhance stakeholder engagement and impact by summarizing feedback from employers, alums, and partners. Importantly, the ethical use of AI must be guided by strong ethics and integrity policies, ensuring transparency, fairness, and compliance with data privacy laws such as FERPA, discussed below. Overall, AI helps institutions develop a QAS that is evidence-based, future-focused, and fairness-minded, aligning local practices and stakeholders' needs while informing accreditation and other reporting requirements.

Step 4: Procedure

To operationalize QAS policies and achieve the desired outcomes, clearly defined procedures must be developed and systematically applied. These procedures should outline the data collection, analysis, and reporting protocols that ensure consistent and accurate evidence across programs. AI tools can support this work by automating data integration from multiple sources (e.g., Title II, CAEP, state reporting), monitoring the validity and reliability of course-embedded assessments, and flagging patterns in candidate performance, retention, and licensure outcomes. AI can be used to strengthen the validity and reliability of locally created assessments by providing systematic, data-driven checks on item performance and scoring practices, as discussed above. Procedurally, programs would upload assessment rubrics and scoring data into an

AI-supported platform; run automated alignment and item analyses and review; review AI-generated reports highlighting validity or reliability concerns; convene faculty or scorer calibration sessions informed by the findings; and document all results, responses, and revisions in the QAS cycle. This creates a transparent, replicable process that uses AI as a decision-support tool while maintaining human oversight for ethical judgment and contextual interpretation (see Figure 5.5).

Identifying procedures for using modeling based on data is essential. Predictive modeling can forecast enrollment, candidate retention, and workforce needs, giving the unit forward-looking evidence to develop responsive and equitable policies. For example, predictive analytics can inform admissions and recruitment policies by identifying underserved

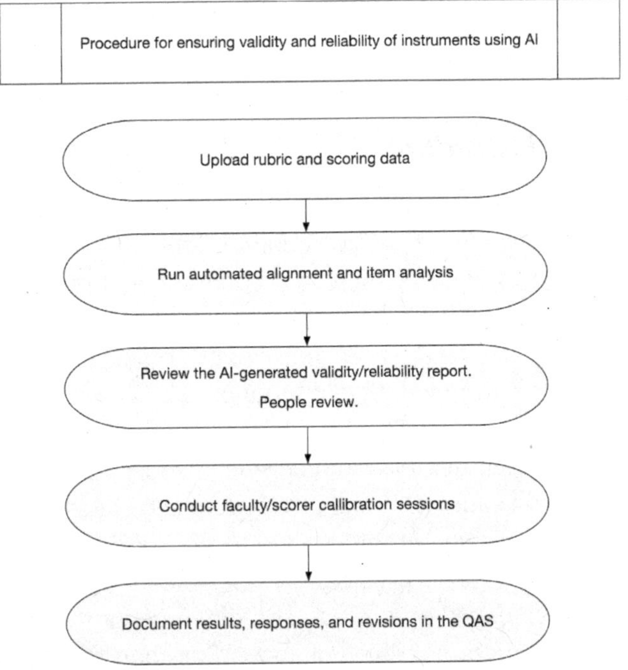

Figure 5.5 Procedures for validity and reliability.

populations. At the same time, scenario modeling can assess how changes in licensure exams, field placements, or financial aid impact candidate success and program compliance. In this way, AI not only supports decision-making but also actively influences policy design, helping institutions anticipate and plan for future demands. Procedures must also define how faculty and staff engage in regular data reviews, including interpreting AI-generated information and verifying its accuracy and relevance. This is an essential component to maintain the "people" component discussed by Krooi et al. (2024). Procedures are informed by and inform policies, dictating the process by which data are used and analyzed, and AI can be critical in defining and analyzing. However, people must be engaged in every aspect (Figure 5.6). Procedures are informed by, while also informing, data and policy, with AI facilitating that process under the watchful eyes of humans.

Additionally, protocols for ethical use of AI, such as protecting privacy, mitigating bias, and ensuring transparency of decision

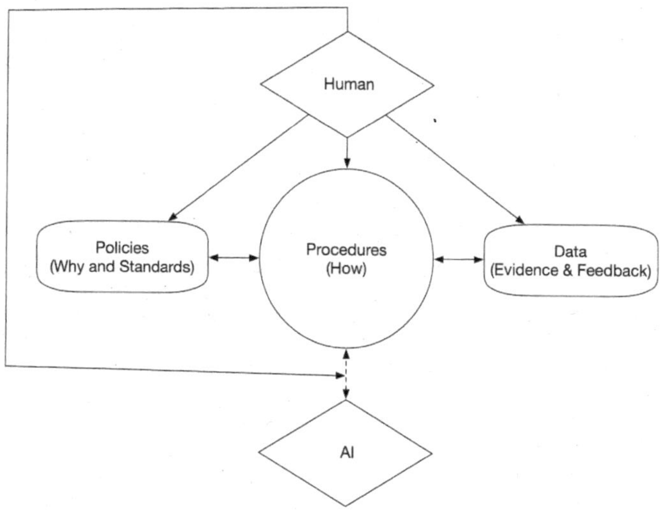

Figure 5.6 Procedures with human interface.

rules, should be embedded into all QAS practices. Finally, procedures should establish feedback loops with stakeholders (P–12 partners, advisory boards, alums, and candidates) to validate findings and inform continuous improvement, ensuring that the QAS remains responsive, evidence-driven, and aligned with accreditation and state/federal requirements.

Chapter 4 discussed the advantages of using AI for accreditation reporting, emphasizing that the following impact of AI is transforming accreditation by streamlining self-study report creation, aligning evidence with standards, and reducing faculty workload.

- Natural Language Processing (NLP) tools, such as ChatGPT, assist in drafting narratives, maintaining consistency, and supporting reflective practice.
- AI-powered mapping accelerates the process mapping across standards (e.g., CAEP, InTASC), utilizing semantic search and machine learning.
- Achieve workload reduction through automation of repetitive tasks, predictive compliance alerts, and AI-generated summaries and dashboards.
- Ethical oversight and human judgment remain essential to ensure AI tools support—not replace—educational integrity and contextual accuracy.

Section 2: Ethical Implications for QAS Design and Continuous Improvement Using AI

The integration of AI into QASs holds great promise for improving efficiency, scalability, and data-informed decision-making. However, the responsible adoption of these technologies requires active human oversight and strong ethical guidance, as discussed in Chapter 2. Human stakeholders, including faculty, staff, advisory boards, and K–12 education partners, provide contextual judgment, nuanced interpretation, and values-based decision-making that AI systems are unable to replicate, often exacerbating misconceptions and biases. This human element ensures that institutional practices remain aligned with the mission, vision, and ethical commitments, increases the accuracy of interpreting results, and mitigates false or biased findings.

Ethical Connections

Crucially, human oversight is necessary to identify and correct errors, biases, and unintended consequences arising from automated data processing. Because AI systems learn patterns from historical data, they risk reproducing and amplifying existing inequities unless carefully monitored. Ongoing human supervision is therefore needed to safeguard fairness in processes such as admissions, assessments, accreditation, and other applications of findings (see Figure 5.7).

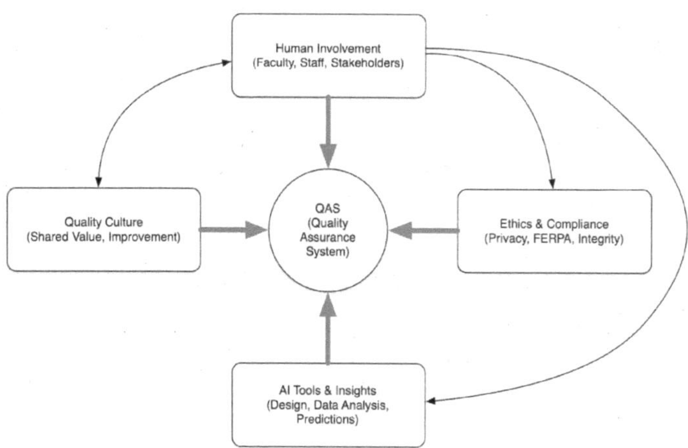

Figure 5.7 Ethical considerations for AI and the QAS.

As highlighted above, two key areas for consideration in QAS and continuous improvement are the use of data and biases (Floridi & Crowls, 2019).

- Data Collection, Consent, and Privacy are essential considerations in any system, and this poses special challenges for AI. Large-scale AI models, especially language models, collect data shared with many users, unaware that their personal information may be archived, analyzed, and utilized in ways they did not explicitly authorize. QASs must be especially cautious not to use AI to analyze non-anatomized data initially gathered for one purpose, as it is often used to train AI for unrelated applications.

- Bias and discrimination in any analysis are a concern. This is primarily a concern for AI, given its reliance on scouring data sources that often lack context and specificity, which can lead to attention being drawn to bias. It also feeds from a confirmation bias structure. Algorithmic bias remains one of the most pressing and complex ethical challenges for artificial intelligence.

Including people in the evaluation of the trustworthiness of a Quality Assurance System (QAS) is essential to ensuring that its design and implementation are not only technically sound but also ethically responsible and contextually relevant. Human evaluators bring unique expertise in interpreting the nuances of program quality, institutional mission, and local educational needs—elements that AI or automated systems alone cannot fully capture. By actively engaging faculty, administrators, students, and external stakeholders in evaluating how data are collected, analyzed, and applied, the institution creates a safeguard against bias, misrepresentation, or overreliance on algorithmic outputs. This human dimension is also critical for protecting sensitive information and ensuring that practices align with ethical frameworks, legal standards such as FERPA, and the broader mission of preparing educators responsibly.

Human involvement in Quality Assurance System (QAS) evaluations is crucial in fostering and maintaining a culture of quality within the unit. As identified by Harvey et al. (2008), a culture of quality goes beyond mere compliance. A culture of quality embodies shared values, practices, and norms among stakeholders who actively participate in the continuous improvement process. When individuals contribute to assessing the trustworthiness of the QAS, they not only confirm the reliability of the findings but also help to build trust, transparency, and accountability within the unit. This collaborative effort creates a supportive QAS framework that is co-created and informed, rather than a top-down mandate, encouraging buy-in from faculty and staff and fostering innovation based on professional expertise. Ultimately, involving people in the evaluation of the QAS is not just an ethical necessity; it represents a strategic approach to nurturing a sustainable culture of quality. In this model, technological tools and human expertise work together to promote continuous improvement and uphold the integrity of educator preparation.

A final, often overlooked, ethical consideration involves vital planning for searching and strategies for using AI to reduce environmental impact. Pilz et al. (2025) in The RAND report titled "AI's Power Requirements Under Exponential Growth," warn that the exponential increase in AI computing could overwhelm both US and global power infrastructures. Global energy demand for AI data centers could approach 327 gigawatts by 2030, with individual training runs requiring as much as eight gigawatts, according to current projections. For reference, 327 gigawatts is approximately 25 percent of the total electricity capacity in the United States today, and comparable to that of the country of Japan. The eight gigawatt training run equals the amount of energy required to power, on average, 2.6 million homes in the United States. In addition, the cooling of AI data center generators requires approximately 700,000 liters of water to "cool" one AI training run, not to mention the pure water needed for the production of the chips and semiconductors used in the processes (Li et al., 2023). The environmental cost of AI is real and needs to be taken into consideration as we move forward with its adoption. Well-planned use of AI can reduce the tax on the system as we develop more efficient ways to use the technology.

Conclusion

While this chapter has outlined the principles and strategic considerations for creating a Quality Assurance System (QAS), many of the detailed models, data matrices, and worked examples are provided on the corresponding website. The website includes full backward design diagrams, crosswalk tables, AI-generated rubric samples, and procedural flowcharts for validity and reliability. These examples are not intended as prescriptive templates, but as practical illustrations of how institutions might adapt the concepts introduced here to their own contexts. Readers seeking deeper technical detail or sample applications are encouraged to consult Appendix A, while the next chapter will return to broader questions of strategy, ethics, and long-term innovation in accreditation.

Grammarly contributed to this text by responding to these AI prompts:

Prompts created by Grammarly
—"Improve it"

Reflection Points

The following questions are designed to help EPPs critically engage with the design and implementation of Quality Assurance Systems (QAS) as tools for both accountability and continuous improvement. These may be used in various ways, including faculty meetings, accreditation planning retreats, and professional learning communities.

Defining Quality and Purpose

- How does your institution currently define "quality" in educator preparation, and how is this definition embedded in your QAS?

- To what extent is your QAS designed for accountability (compliance with accreditation) versus improvement (supporting innovation and growth)?

- How might you balance these dual purposes more effectively?

Evidence and Data Use

- What types of data (quantitative, qualitative, or mixed) are most central to your QAS?

- How is disaggregated data currently being used to identify and address equity gaps in candidate performance or program outcomes?

- Where might AI tools enhance your ability to analyze complex evidence, while ensuring transparency and validity?

Faculty and Stakeholder Engagement

- How are faculty, staff, and candidates engaged in shaping your QAS processes?

- In what ways does your QAS reflect the voices of external partners, such as P–12 school leaders, employers, or alums?

- What additional structures might foster more authentic stakeholder participation in accreditation and improvement cycles?

Decision-Making and Governance

- What processes ensure that QAS findings directly inform program decision-making?

- Are there "episodes of decision-making" in which compliance requirements have sidelined faculty judgment? If so, how could this balance be restored?

- What governance structures would build confidence in the fairness, transparency, and effectiveness of QAS processes?

Ethical and Equity Considerations

- How does your QAS ensure that continuous improvement efforts prioritize equity, inclusivity, and candidate success across diverse demographics?

- What safeguards are in place to avoid the misuse or misinterpretation of data in high-stakes accreditation contexts?

- How could ethical principles guide the integration of AI, predictive modeling, or other emerging technologies in QAS processes?

Beyond Continuous Improvement— Strategic Innovation

- How might your QAS be leveraged not only for compliance but also for institutional innovation and leadership in educator preparation?

- What "next steps" could move your QAS from cyclical reporting to a dynamic, real-time system of continuous feedback and adaptation?

- How could your institution use scenario planning or predictive analytics to anticipate future accreditation requirements and position itself proactively?

6 Strategic and Ethical Implementation of AI in Accreditation

Introduction

Artificial Intelligence (AI) has emerged as a transformative force in higher education, with particular relevance to the processes of accreditation and quality assurance. At its best, AI can serve as a catalyst for strengthening institutional effectiveness and accountability. Accreditation can be measurably improved when institutions integrate credible data pipelines, role-based AI literacy, enforceable governance frameworks, and human-in-the-loop safeguards that ensure transparency and fairness (Pearson & Monaco, 2025; Council for Higher Education Accreditation International Quality Group [CHEA], 2025). Under these conditions, AI enables accreditation to move beyond compliance reporting toward a culture of continuous improvement, where evidence synthesis is accelerated, alignment to standards is more precise, and time is freed for meaningful reflection and collaboration.

At the same time, the potential of AI in accreditation carries profound risks if implemented without care. While AI can streamline documentation, provide real-time insights, and support decision-making, overreliance on these tools can result in bias, deskilling, and the erosion of trust in accreditation systems. These dangers are compounded by threats to data security, the possibility of hallucinated or inaccurate outputs, and the displacement of authentic institutional reflection in favor of algorithmic shortcuts (Morris, 2025; Southern Association of Colleges and Schools Commission on Colleges

[SACSCOC], 2024). Thus, the challenge for institutions is not whether to integrate AI into accreditation, but how to do so responsibly and strategically.

This chapter addresses this challenge by outlining the conditions under which AI can enhance rather than undermine the accreditation process. Specifically, we will—

- Examine AI literacy for faculty and administrators, emphasizing why professional development is essential for ensuring AI is used accurately and responsibly.
- Turn to governance and ethical policy frameworks, highlighting principles such as transparency, accountability, privacy, and human oversight that must underpin AI adoption.
- Explore cross-institutional and collaborative dimensions, considering how partnerships, peer review, and shared guidelines can strengthen adoption.
- Analyze barriers to AI implementation, including technical, cultural, and ethical challenges, as well as strategies for overcoming them.
- Present case applications and examples that demonstrate how institutions are already deploying AI in accreditation contexts across diverse professional domains.

Together, these sections provide a roadmap for the strategic and ethical implementation of AI in accreditation, offering both a critical lens and a practical framework for institutional leaders navigating this evolving landscape.

Building AI Literacy in Accreditation

The successful integration of AI into accreditation requires technical infrastructure and robust AI literacy among faculty, administrators, and accreditation staff. Without intentional preparation, institutions risk misapplying AI tools, overlooking errors, or allowing automation to displace human judgment. Building capacity across roles ensures that AI enhances institutional effectiveness rather than undermining it.

Faculty and Administrator Capacity-Building

One important dimension of AI literacy is the ability to leverage AI for managing the complexity of accreditation standards. In nursing education, for example, AI supports faculty credential tracking, curriculum mapping, and alignment with competency-based standards, allowing programs to remain agile in rapidly evolving fields such as healthcare (Morris, 2025). By embedding these tools in program oversight, institutions can monitor compliance in real time while ensuring that curricular content remains aligned with external benchmarks.

For administrators, training in AI-enabled dashboards and predictive analytics is essential. These platforms consolidate data from multiple sources, offering leaders visibility into retention trends, faculty qualifications, and potential compliance gaps. Staff equipped to interpret and act on these dashboards can move from reactive reporting to proactive strategic improvement (NIU College Trade School Articles, 2025). Similarly, AI-driven documentation tools automate the collation of evidence portfolios, freeing staff from the burdens of manual data entry and enabling them instead to focus on evaluating institutional effectiveness.

Yet capacity-building must go beyond technical proficiency. Effective training requires a critical dimension of AI literacy: staff must be prepared to recognize and correct AI "hallucinations," validate outputs against institutional knowledge, and preserve human oversight in decision-making processes (Bisoux, 2024; Pearson & Monaco, 2025). Without this critical awareness, institutions risk embedding inaccuracies into official reports, undermining credibility with accreditors. Faculty and administrators alike must therefore develop habits of verification and collaborative review to ensure the integrity of AI-supported accreditation work.

AI Literacy as an Ethical Necessity

AI literacy is not simply a functional requirement; it is also an ethical necessity. Educators and administrators must understand how to evaluate AI outputs for bias, privacy implications, and accuracy to safeguard institutional trust and uphold accreditation integrity (Pearson & Monaco, 2025). As AI tools increasingly rely on sensitive institutional and student data, literacy in data privacy and responsible use becomes central to both compliance and professional responsibility.

Faculty development aligned to accreditation and professional standards is also essential. In fields such as nursing and healthcare, faculty must remain current in how AI tools are reshaping accreditation requirements and professional practice expectations (Morris, 2025). Continuous professional development ensures that faculty are equipped to integrate AI responsibly while maintaining the human-centered values— mentorship, empathy, and professional judgment—that accreditation processes are designed to protect.

Taken together, AI literacy in accreditation contexts requires institutions to train staff at multiple levels: technical proficiency in dashboards and automation, critical skills in identifying and correcting errors, and ethical awareness of privacy, bias, and equity implications. This multilayered approach enables AI to serve as an accelerator of quality assurance and continuous improvement, while protecting accreditation from the risks of overreliance and misuse.

Governance and Ethical Policy Frameworks for AI in Accreditation

The transformative potential of AI in accreditation can only be realized when its use is guided by governance structures that ensure fairness, transparency, and accountability. Without enforceable guardrails, institutions risk undermining both the credibility of accreditation processes and the trust of their stakeholders. Strong governance provides the foundation for balancing innovation with responsibility, ensuring that AI is deployed in ways that augment rather than distort institutional effectiveness.

Principles of AI Use

At the most fundamental level, accrediting organizations have articulated core principles for the responsible use of AI. The Council for Higher Education Accreditation International Quality Group (CHEA) emphasizes that human decision-making must remain central, with AI positioned as a supportive tool rather than a substitute for human judgment. CHEA further highlights the importance of using only verifiable data and upholding transparency in AI-driven processes to prevent manipulation or misrepresentation of evidence (CHEA, 2025).

The Southern Association of Colleges and Schools Commission on Colleges (SACSCOC) expands on these principles by underscoring the need for confidentiality, security, and verifiability in all accreditation submissions. SACSCOC warns against overreliance on generative AI models, given their risks of producing hallucinated or fabricated information that, if unchecked, could erode the validity of accreditation reports (SACSCOC, 2024). These guidelines frame governance not only as a procedural matter but as an ethical imperative to protect institutional integrity.

Institutional Frameworks

At the institutional level, governance requires policies that address the ethical and secure use of AI in accreditation workflows. Within educator preparation programs, for example, policies must explicitly address data privacy, bias mitigation, and AI system security to safeguard both candidate and student information (Pearson & Monaco, 2025). Such frameworks ensure that accreditation evidence remains reliable and compliant with broader legal and professional obligations.

SACSCOC also reminds institutions that accreditation is not solely a technical exercise; it is a reflective process designed to strengthen institutional learning. Governance frameworks must therefore ensure that AI supports—but does not replace—the authentic dialogue and collaboration that occur during self-study and peer review (SACSCOC, 2024). Without such safeguards, institutions risk allowing automation to erode the developmental value of accreditation as a process of institutional reflection and improvement.

Similarly, the Council for the Accreditation of Educator Preparation (CAEP) has emphasized the importance of embedding AI within educator preparation programs through structured frameworks that prioritize privacy, equity, and reflective practice. CAEP's guidance highlights that while AI can streamline evidence gathering and support instructional planning, its integration must be accompanied by policies that safeguard personally identifiable information, address bias in AI outputs, and reinforce faculty development (Pearson & Monaco, 2025). In this view, governance extends to preparing faculty and candidates to critically evaluate AI outputs, engage in collaborative reflection, and ensure that human judgment remains central.

Ethical Guardrails

Governance also entails the creation of ongoing ethical guardrails to monitor the performance of AI systems. Institutions must engage in continuous auditing of AI tools to ensure that their outputs remain accurate, equitable, and aligned with accrediting standards (Pearson & Monaco, 2025). Regular review processes help identify and mitigate algorithmic bias, which, if left unchecked, could skew accreditation reporting and disadvantage particular groups of students or programs.

In nursing education, for instance, continuous monitoring of AI-driven dashboards and predictive analytics is critical to ensuring that compliance tracking remains fair and reliable. Faculty oversight and human review of AI outputs provide an additional safeguard for maintaining the integrity of accreditation evidence (Morris, 2025). By embedding auditing practices into their governance frameworks, institutions not only strengthen trust in their accreditation processes but also signal their commitment to ethical AI use.

Cross-Institutional and Collaborative Dimensions

The implementation of AI in accreditation cannot be treated as an isolated institutional effort. Because accreditation is inherently a relational process involving institutions, accrediting bodies, and peer reviewers, AI adoption must be shaped by collaborative frameworks. Partnerships and shared learning across organizations help establish norms for ethical use, reduce duplication of effort, and build collective trust in AI-enabled practices.

Inter-Organizational Collaboration

Institutions benefit significantly from partnering with accreditation experts and consultants who can guide them in responsibly implementing AI tools. These experts help align AI platforms with accreditor-specific standards, frameworks, and documentation preferences, ensuring that technology does not operate at odds with established expectations (NIU College Trade School Articles, 2025). Consultants also provide training and compliance audits that contextualize AI use within each accreditor's unique culture, reducing risks of misalignment.

Beyond individual partnerships, multi-campus and international collaboration plays a critical role in shaping shared understandings of ethical AI use. CHEA emphasizes that accrediting organizations and institutions must work together to uphold human oversight, data integrity, and transparency in AI practices. Collaborative networks that cross national and institutional boundaries enable stakeholders to exchange lessons learned, codify responsible practices, and define guardrails for using AI in quality assurance (CHEA, 2025). Such efforts extend the benefits of AI adoption beyond single campuses and contribute to a global dialogue on trust and accountability in accreditation.

Collaborative Learning and Faculty Development

Collaboration is equally vital at the faculty level. AI literacy and ethical integration are strengthened when institutions establish mechanisms for peer review of AI-generated outputs, ensuring that automated reports or dashboards are validated for accuracy, contextual fit, and integrity (Morris, 2025). These peer review practices not only protect against errors but also preserve the human judgment central to accreditation.

At a structural level, institutions can embed collaboration through the creation of task forces, advisory boards, and working groups dedicated to AI in education and accreditation. Within educator preparation programs, such collaborative bodies serve as spaces where faculty, administrators, and external stakeholders collectively review AI policies, assess emerging tools, and update frameworks in response to evolving risks and opportunities (Pearson & Monaco, 2025). By engaging diverse perspectives, these groups ensure that institutional AI strategies are not only technically sound but also reflective of professional values and ethical commitments.

In sum, cross-institutional and collaborative approaches create a network of accountability, dialogue, and shared expertise. These partnerships, whether external with accreditors and consultants or internal through faculty peer review and task forces, are essential to building responsible, sustainable, and trustworthy AI integration in accreditation.

Overcoming Barriers to Adoption

While the promise of AI in accreditation is substantial, its effective implementation requires institutions to overcome significant technical, cultural, and ethical barriers. Without deliberate strategies to address these obstacles, AI adoption risks deepening inequities, diminishing human judgment, and eroding trust in accreditation processes.

Technical Barriers

One of the most pressing challenges is the uneven technological readiness of institutions. Many higher education providers continue to rely on manual compliance processes—such as spreadsheets and fragmented databases—that cannot match the efficiency, precision, or adaptability of AI-driven ecosystems

(NIU College Trade School Articles, 2025). These outdated systems place institutions at a disadvantage, leaving them less agile in responding to evolving accreditation requirements and unable to generate real-time insights that support continuous improvement.

Cultural and Human Barriers

Even when technical systems are in place, cultural and human factors present significant hurdles. As Morris (2025) observes, the risk of overreliance on AI threatens to diminish the human elements of accreditation, including faculty judgment, creativity, and empathy—qualities central to professional fields like nursing education. Accreditation is not only about compliance but also about institutional reflection and dialogue, processes that cannot be automated without loss of meaning.

Resistance to adoption also stems from concerns about academic integrity, data privacy, and accuracy. Faculty and administrators may be reluctant to trust AI tools when generative systems are known to produce hallucinations, fabricate data, or reproduce biased outputs (Morris, 2025; SACSCOC, 2024). Similarly, fears about breaches of confidentiality and the misuse of sensitive institutional data can undermine willingness to integrate AI into accreditation workflows. These concerns highlight the importance of building both technical safeguards and cultural confidence in AI systems.

Strategies to Overcome Barriers

Addressing these barriers requires a deliberate and systemic approach. First, institutions must embed AI literacy within accreditation training. Faculty and administrators should be equipped with the technical skills to operate AI tools along with capacities to validate outputs, recognize hallucinations, and maintain human oversight in decision-making (Bisoux, 2024; Pearson & Monaco, 2025). By framing AI literacy as both a technical and ethical necessity, institutions can ensure that AI complements rather than supplants professional judgment.

Second, institutions must commit to institutionalizing secure, transparent, and human-centered governance frameworks. CHEA (2025) underscores the importance of transparency and human control in decision-making, while Pearson and Monaco (2025) stress that policies addressing data privacy, security, and bias mitigation are foundational for trust. By embedding these principles into institutional frameworks, colleges and universities can reassure stakeholders that AI systems are deployed responsibly and aligned with the values of fairness, accountability, and continuous improvement.

Case Applications and Examples

The application of AI in accreditation is not theoretical—it is already being tested across diverse professional domains. These case studies illustrate how institutions are leveraging AI to accelerate compliance, streamline reporting, and strengthen continuous improvement. At the same time, they highlight the ethical, governance, and literacy safeguards necessary to ensure AI augments rather than undermines accreditation processes.

Business School Accreditation

Business schools have been among the early adopters of generative AI for accreditation, especially in streamlining AACSB processes. Tools such as chatbots provide administrators with quick, structured outputs from complex data sets. However, accuracy and human oversight remain essential.

- Application of AI chatbots:
  - Calculate faculty course coverage (e.g., SA vs. adjunct balance).
  - Summarize faculty publications and categorize by discipline.
  - Compile mission-based activity summaries (e.g., community service, internships).
- Key safeguard: Validate all outputs for accuracy and completeness to prevent hallucinations (Bisoux, 2024).

Nursing Accreditation

Nursing programs face increasing complexity due to evolving healthcare standards and competency-based models. AI has been deployed to provide continuous monitoring of compliance metrics and support program agility, ensuring quality while reducing faculty burden.

- Application of AI tools:
  - Real-time dashboards tracking accreditation metrics.
  - Competency monitoring to ensure alignment with AACN and other standards.
  - Predictive analytics to identify at-risk students early.
  - Automated reporting to streamline compliance submissions.
- **Key safeguard**: Balance efficiency with the human touch of mentorship and empathy (Morris, 2025).

Educator Preparation

Educator preparation programs are beginning to craft AI integration frameworks that align directly with CAEP and InTASC standards. These frameworks emphasize not only compliance but also ethical practice, equity safeguards, and professional reflection for faculty and candidates.

- AI Frameworks from CAEP and InTASC standards:
  - Protect data privacy and candidate/student PII.
  - Audit outputs for bias and accuracy.
  - Embed AI literacy into curricula and clinical experiences.
  - Promote equity safeguards and human oversight in all applications.
- Key safeguard: Ensure AI supports reflection, ethics, and equity in educator preparation (Pearson & Monaco, 2025).

Consultancy Partnerships

Many institutions are turning to external accreditation experts to guide AI adoption. Consultants bring specialized knowledge of accreditor-specific requirements, pairing technical solutions with training and audits that ensure readiness across multiple accreditation bodies.

- Consultant uses of AI:
  - Select and implement AI platforms aligned to accreditor standards.
  - Provide staff training on dashboards, predictive analytics, and documentation.
  - Conduct compliance audits to identify gaps and risks.
  - Reduce administrative burden while maintaining continuous readiness.
- Key safeguard: Align all tools with specific accreditor frameworks and expectations (NIU College Trade School Articles, 2025).

Taken together, these cases underscore the central thesis of this chapter: AI can measurably improve the quality and efficiency of accreditation when institutions combine credible data pipelines with role-based literacy, enforceable governance, and human oversight. Across business, nursing, educator preparation, and consultancy models, the evidence points to AI's ability to accelerate evidence synthesis, enhance alignment with standards, and free faculty for authentic reflection. Yet the same examples also illustrate the risks of bias, deskilling, and erosion of trust if AI is deployed without transparency, safeguards, and continuous human judgment. By adopting frameworks that prioritize accuracy, equity, and ethical governance, institutions can ensure that AI functions not as a substitute for professional reflection, but as a catalyst for deeper continuous improvement in accreditation (Bisoux, 2024; Morris, 2025; NIU College Trade School Articles, 2025; Pearson & Monaco, 2025; SACSCOC, 2024; CHEA, 2025).

Conclusion

Accreditation is most effective when it is a process of authentic reflection, grounded in evidence and shared dialogue across an institution. Artificial Intelligence offers tools to reduce burdensome documentation, accelerate evidence synthesis, and provide real-time insights that strengthen alignment with standards. Yet, as this chapter has emphasized, AI can reduce performative compliance and strengthen continuous improvement only if institutions integrate role-based AI literacy, enforceable governance frameworks, collaborative structures, and human-in-the-loop safeguards (Pearson & Monaco, 2025).

At its core, AI must augment—not replace—human judgment. Overreliance on automated systems risks diminishing the creativity, empathy, and professional discernment that make accreditation meaningful. Safeguards that prioritize privacy, transparency, and equity are therefore essential to ensuring that AI serves as a catalyst rather than a constraint in accreditation processes (SACSCOC, 2024; Morris, 2025).

Looking ahead, institutions that adopt transparent, ethical, and collaborative AI frameworks will be positioned to lead in the next era of accreditation. By embedding AI thoughtfully—aligned with guiding principles of fairness, accountability, and human oversight—colleges and universities can not only meet accreditor expectations but also model a culture of continuous quality improvement. In doing so, they advance accreditation beyond compliance into a driver of institutional excellence and innovation (Council for Higher Education Accreditation, 2025; Pearson & Monaco, 2025).

In closing, it is important to acknowledge that the recurring emphasis in this book on human engagement, ethical practice, and the role of AI as a supportive tool rather than a replacement was deliberate. These themes are the anchors of responsible innovation in accreditation. Just as accreditation itself requires continual reevaluation of evidence, values, and outcomes, this book has repeatedly returned to these principles to underscore their centrality. Keeping ethics and human judgment at the forefront ensures that AI serves as a catalyst for equity and improvement, rather than a distraction from the professional wisdom and integrity that define educator preparation.

Reflection Points

The following questions are designed to help educator preparation programs consider how to strategically implement AI in accreditation contexts. These questions may be used for individual reflection, team discussions, or as part of institutional planning and professional development activities.

Faculty and Administrator Preparedness

- What is the current level of AI literacy among your faculty and staff?
- What kinds of professional development would best prepare your community for ethical and effective AI adoption?

Governance and Policy

- What policies exist (or are missing) in your institution regarding AI use in accreditation and quality assurance?
- How might governance structures ensure transparency and accountability in AI-driven processes?

Ethical Integration

- How does your institution ensure that AI adoption aligns with the principles of fairness, equity, and inclusion?
- What mechanisms could be put in place to monitor bias and unintended consequences of AI systems?

Cross-Institutional Collaboration

- What opportunities exist for collaboration with peer institutions to share resources, policies, or AI implementation strategies?
- How could such collaborations reduce costs and improve consistency in accreditation outcomes?

Overcoming Barriers

- What cultural, financial, or technical barriers might impede AI adoption at your institution?

- How might leadership address these barriers while maintaining trust and faculty engagement?

7 Transformative Innovations and the Future of AI

Introduction

Artificial Intelligence (AI) is no longer a speculative addition to teacher preparation; it is an active force reshaping how educator preparation programs (EPPs) engage in accreditation, quality assurance, and continuous improvement. Throughout this book, we have examined AI's role in data-driven decision-making, ethical challenges, episodes of bias mitigation, and applied practices. This concluding chapter brings those threads together to envision how these themes converge in the broader transformation of accreditation processes and their implications for faculty, students, accrediting bodies, and policymakers.

Accreditation has historically operated through cyclical reviews, bureaucratic documentation, and retrospective evaluations. However, AI introduces a paradigm shift toward continuous improvement, predictive evaluation, and dynamic alignment with equity and workforce outcomes (Annuš, 2024). With tools such as machine learning, natural language generation, and real-time data dashboards, accreditation bodies and educator preparation programs (EPPs) can move beyond compliance-driven reporting toward proactive, ethically grounded, and innovation-oriented systems (U.S. Department of Education, 2023). The shift underscores not only efficiency but also institutional agency: faculty and leaders become co-creators in shaping how AI enhances accreditation, rather than passive adopters of technological change.

Integration with Earlier Chapters

This chapter builds upon themes introduced earlier in the book. Chapter 1 established the historical foundations of accreditation and framed the initial promises and risks of AI in education. It set the stage for understanding accreditation not only as a compliance mechanism but also as a driver of educational quality. Building on that foundation, Chapter 2 examined AI in data-driven decision-making, showing how predictive analytics and real-time monitoring enhance accreditation practices. Chapter 3 extended this conversation by focusing on ethical concerns, particularly issues of bias, fairness, and human oversight in high-stakes decision-making. Chapter 4 explored how AI reshapes one of the most resource-intensive aspects of accreditation—self-study report writing and evidence mapping, while Chapter 5 provided applied practices that illustrate how these tools are implemented in day-to-day accreditation workflows. Finally, Chapter 6 emphasized continuous improvement and the transition toward deeper strategic innovation, situating AI as a catalyst for cultural and structural change.

Taken together, these explorations show how momentary decisions—whether to trust an algorithm's recommendation, adjust faculty review processes, or design a bias check—accumulate into long-term transformation. Chapter 7 therefore serves as a capstone, stressing continuity between past innovations and the future possibilities of AI-driven accreditation.

AI for Systems-Level Change in Teacher Preparation

AI supports a systemic reimagination of teacher preparation, enabling accreditation models that are both responsive and proactive. By leveraging learning analytics and predictive modeling, EPPs can align curriculum delivery, candidate development, and licensure readiness with broader institutional and societal needs (Zawacki-Richter et al., 2019; Wang & Xing, 2024). AI-enhanced systems allow for seamless data-sharing between EPPs, K–12 schools, and accreditation agencies—building real-time interoperability that eliminates data silos and accelerates continuous improvement cycles (Prinsloo et al., 2021; Johnson et al., 2024).

Competency-based accreditation models are emerging as a significant innovation, empowered by AI tools that assess candidate performance across domains such as cultural competence, adaptive instruction, and reflective practice. Edwards et al. (2025) propose AI-supported systems that update performance metrics dynamically, moving accreditation away from static compliance toward transformative educational outcomes.

Generative AI for Accreditation Documentation and Feedback

One of the most immediate applications of AI in accreditation is the use of generative AI tools—such as OpenAI's Generative Pre-trained Transformer 4 (GPT-4)—to assist with writing self-study narratives, standards alignment matrices, and evidence-based reflections. These tools help EPPs produce high-quality documentation efficiently, alleviating some of the faculty workload that traditionally accompanies accreditation cycles (Kelly & Smith, 2024; Zhai et al., 2021).

Natural language generation platforms are now being piloted to draft documentation aligned with national standards, enabling faculty to focus more on content quality and less on formatting and compliance. Ifenthaler and Yau (2020) developed the Evaluation of Learning Outcomes System (EVALLOS), an intelligent platform that automates both Program Learning Outcome and Course Learning Outcome alignment reporting, detects anomalies, and supports compliance during accreditation reviews. The system also streamlines assessment and AI-driven reporting, significantly enhancing efficiency in accreditation-related tasks.

Equity by Design: Building Fair Accreditation Systems

The integration of AI into accreditation processes must be guided by principles of fairness, transparency, and accountability. Left unchecked, algorithms can encode and amplify biases in educational data. Prinsloo et al. (2021) emphasize the necessity of responsible AI governance frameworks that include bias audits, explainability protocols, and inclusive stakeholder engagement.

Williamson (2019) introduced the Dynamic AI Governance in Education model, which outlines indicators such as transparency, agency, and impact monitoring that accreditation bodies can adopt to mitigate algorithmic bias. Johnson et al. (2024) similarly argue that equity-focused AI must be audited at every stage—data input, processing, and reporting—to prevent systemic marginalization of historically underrepresented candidates.

Faculty Empowerment and Human-Centered AI

Rather than replacing faculty expertise, AI must serve as an augmentation tool. Faculty remain central to the ethical, pedagogical, and contextual interpretation of accreditation evidence. Cooper et al. (2025) found that faculty confidence in using generative AI increases when institutions provide structured training in prompt engineering, bias identification, and ethical safeguards.

A systematic review by Masoumian Hosseini et al. (2025) underscores that faculty adoption of AI tools is most successful when paired with professional development programs focused on responsible AI use. Viberg et al. (2023) emphasize participatory design approaches that allow faculty to shape the development of AI systems, reinforcing trust and enhancing tool relevance.

AI for Predictive and Real-Time Continuous Improvement

Traditional accreditation models often rely on decennial reviews that provide limited insight into ongoing program health. AI enables real-time data dashboards and predictive analytics that can alert faculty to emerging issues such as candidate attrition, declining assessment scores, or mentor evaluations (Wang & Xing, 2024). These tools allow for proactive remediation and evidence-based strategy adjustments.

EVALLOS illustrates how AI can automate alignment between institutional performance and accreditation criteria, enabling continuous improvement (Ifenthaler & Yau, 2020). Similarly, Triana et al. (2024) describe Colombia's engineering programs using AI-supported data governance to align institutional metrics with national quality assurance benchmarks.

Balancing Tensions in AI and Accreditation

As the preceding chapters reveal, the integration of AI in accreditation is not a story of uniform consensus, but of productive tensions. These differing emphases highlight the dual nature of AI: a source of new possibilities, and a reminder of the enduring responsibilities that define educator preparation. Addressing these tensions head-on is essential for a balanced and credible vision of the future (See Table 7.1).

Table 7.1 Tension in AI and Accreditation

Tension	Advantage Emphasis	Caution Emphasis
Efficiency vs. Authenticity	AI reduces workload by automating evidence mapping, reports, and compliance (Chs. 1, 2, 4, 5, 6, 7).	Risk of shallow compliance or loss of reflective authenticity if efficiency dominates (Chs. 3, 4).
Transformational vs. Supportive	AI reframes accreditation as a systemic paradigm shift with predictive/global potential (Chs. 1, 2, 7).	AI must remain a decision-support tool, never replacing human judgment (Chs. 3, 5).
Equity as Promise vs. Equity as Risk	Dashboards and predictive tools can surface disparities and promote fairness (Chs. 1, 2, 5, 6).	AI may reproduce inequities if trained on biased data or global benchmarks (Chs. 3, 7).
Faculty Burden Reduction vs. New Responsibilities	Automation frees faculty from repetitive reporting, supporting reflective practice (Chs. 1, 2, 4, 5).	Faculty must adopt oversight, AI literacy, and governance responsibilities (Chs. 3, 6, 7).
Incremental vs. Predictive Continuous Improvement	AI supports incremental improvement cycles via dashboards and QAS monitoring (Chs. 1, 2, 5, 6).	The shift to predictive, real-time, global improvement raises challenges of scope and oversight (Ch. 7).

Efficiency Versus Authenticity

AI can dramatically reduce the administrative workload of accreditation by automating evidence mapping, report drafting, and compliance monitoring (Chapters 1, 2, 4, 5, 6, and 7). Yet, as cautioned in Chapters 3 and 4, efficiency must not come at the expense of reflective practice. The balance lies in using efficiency to free faculty time for deeper reflection and authentic engagement, not to bypass it.

AI as Transformational Versus Supportive Tool

Some chapters cast AI as a paradigm shift capable of reimagining accreditation systems globally (Chapters 1, 2, and 7), while others stress its role as a supportive tool requiring human oversight (Chapters 3 and 5). Both are true: AI is transformational in scope, but only if implemented as a human-centered support system rather than a substitute for judgment.

Equity as Promise Versus Equity as Risk

AI offers powerful mechanisms for surfacing disparities and ensuring accountability in recruitment, progression, and completion data (Chapters 1, 2, 5, and 6). At the same time, if trained on biased or incomplete data, AI may reproduce inequities (Chapters 3 and 7). The lesson is clear: equity is not an automatic outcome of AI adoption but a conditional promise—realized only through governance, diverse datasets, and intentional design.

Faculty Burden Reduction Versus New Responsibilities

Faculty experience both relief and added demands in an AI-enhanced accreditation process. While repetitive reporting tasks are automated (Chapters 1, 2, 4, and 5), new responsibilities emerge around oversight, AI literacy, and ethical judgment (Chapters 3, 6, and 7). The shift is not toward less faculty involvement, but toward different involvement—less clerical labor, more strategic and ethical stewardship.

Continuous Improvement: Incremental Versus Predictive

Chapters highlight continuous improvement at multiple scales: incremental adjustments within QAS cycles (Chapters 1, 2, 5, and 6), and predictive, systemic improvement enabled by real-time analytics and global benchmarking (Chapter 7). These are not contradictory models but points along a trajectory: AI enables continuous improvement to evolve from local and incremental to predictive and systemic.

Tensions as a Source of Balance

These tensions should not be seen as contradictions but as balancing forces that keep accreditation credible. Efficiency is tempered by authenticity, transformation by oversight, equity by vigilance, empowerment by responsibility, and incremental improvement by predictive horizons. Together, these balances illustrate that the future of accreditation will not be defined by AI alone, but by the dynamic interplay of technological innovation and human judgment.

Global Trends and Benchmarking in Accreditation AI

Globally, countries are experimenting with AI-powered accreditation models that prioritize equity, transparency, and global comparability. Nordic countries have adopted centralized AI dashboards to support teacher education quality assurance (Viberg et al., 2023), while international bodies like United Nations Educational, Scientific, and Cultural Organization (UNESCO) and the Organization for Economic Co-operation and Development (OECD) provide ethical guidelines to safeguard AI adoption in education.

Zawacki-Richter et al. (2019) caution, however, that global benchmarking should be approached carefully to avoid reproducing colonial evaluation systems. Accreditation frameworks must be culturally situated, ensuring AI tools reflect local values, pedagogies, and educational priorities.

Recommendations and Research Agenda

To fully realize the potential of AI in accreditation, several priorities emerge. First, EPPs and accreditors must embed fairness, explainability, and transparency into all AI systems. Second, faculty should be trained and supported as AI collaborators, not passive tool users. Third, research on long-term outcomes—such as educator effectiveness and program equity—must be sustained to validate AI's efficacy.

Finally, accreditation bodies should consider adopting frameworks that integrate principles of datafication, automation, and international governance of education, as discussed by Williamson (2019), or responsible AI protocols (Prinsloo et al., 2021) to create systems that are agile, equitable, and globally informed. As Annuš (2024) notes, the future of accreditation—and education broadly—depends on a thoughtful balance between algorithmic capabilities and human professional judgment.

Future Ethical Dilemmas

Ethics has been a recurring theme across this book, but the future of accreditation raises new dilemmas. For example, as generative AI becomes increasingly capable, institutions may be tempted to rely on it to draft self-study reports or accreditation narratives. While efficient, such practices risk diminishing human judgment and critical reflection.

Another dilemma is inequity: well-resourced EPPs may have the capacity to implement sophisticated AI systems, while smaller or underfunded institutions may be left behind. This creates a risk of uneven playing fields in demonstrating quality and compliance.

Global frameworks, such as UNESCO's (2021) guidance on AI in education, point toward the need for shared ethical standards. Similarly, US Department of Education (2023) reports stress transparency, accountability, and human oversight. Building international consensus around ethical AI in accreditation will help prevent both overreliance on automation and systemic inequities.

Beyond Continuous Improvement— Strategic Innovation

Throughout accreditation history, continuous improvement has been framed as incremental: reviewing outcomes, making small adjustments, and reporting progress in cycles. AI, however, allows for a shift toward strategic innovation.

AI-powered scenario modeling can simulate "what-if" possibilities, such as the impact of new licensure requirements or changes in teacher workforce demands. Predictive analytics can benchmark performance against national and international standards, encouraging cross-institutional comparisons. With these capabilities, accreditation can evolve from a compliance-oriented activity into a proactive system of strategic design.

Rather than reacting to standards, EPPs can anticipate them, demonstrating leadership in shaping the field of teacher preparation.

Stakeholder Perspectives

The AI-driven transformation of accreditation will be experienced differently by various stakeholders:

- **Faculty** may find their administrative burden reduced, but will take on new responsibilities for ethical oversight and critical interpretation of AI outputs.

- **Students** stand to benefit from earlier interventions and personalized supports, ensuring equitable opportunities for success.

- **Accrediting bodies** will gain access to real-time, standardized evidence, allowing them to focus on program quality rather than compliance checklists.

- **Policymakers** will see stronger evidence for decision-making about teacher workforce readiness.

- **Employers** may begin to rely more heavily on AI-enhanced accreditation reports when evaluating the credibility of teacher preparation programs.

By considering these perspectives, institutions can ensure that the integration of AI into accreditation is not only efficient but also inclusive and context-sensitive.

Global Context

While accreditation processes have traditionally been national or regional, AI introduces possibilities for global collaboration. UNESCO (2021) has emphasized the importance of international cooperation in the governance of AI and education. With AI-enabled benchmarking and data-sharing, institutions may one day participate in cross-national quality assurance systems that transcend traditional borders.

Such global frameworks could encourage harmonized teacher preparation standards, ensuring that educators are equipped for increasingly interconnected classrooms. This also highlights the potential for AI to bridge—not widen—global inequities in teacher preparation, if implemented with fairness at the core.

Conclusion and Call to Action

As this book concludes, one central message emerges: Educator Preparation Programs (EPPs) must not merely adopt AI but actively shape its role in accreditation. The uncertainties surrounding AI—ranging from data ethics to global inequities—are not obstacles but opportunities for leadership and innovation.

Faculty, administrators, accrediting bodies, and policymakers are co-creators of this future. They must ensure that AI is embedded ethically, equitably, and innovatively into accreditation systems. Doing so requires vigilance against bias, a commitment to transparency, and a reaffirmation of human judgment as the final authority in high-stakes decisions. At the same time, EPPs must cultivate the imagination to move beyond a narrow vision of "continuous improvement" toward truly transformative innovation.

Accreditation is not simply about compliance; it is about preparing educators to meet the challenges of tomorrow. In this mission, AI should not be seen as a substitute for human expertise but as a partner. Used wisely, it has the potential to create accreditation systems that are more efficient, rigorous, and just—systems that foreground equity, anticipate emerging workforce needs, and remain globally connected.

The integration of AI into accreditation processes thus presents both transformative opportunities and profound challenges. As discussed throughout this book, frameworks grounded in datafication, automation, and responsible governance (Williamson & Eynon, 2020; UNESCO, 2021; U.S. Department of Education, 2023) offer pathways for ensuring that AI adoption remains ethical, transparent, and inclusive. By pairing algorithmic capabilities with human professional judgment, accreditation can move from episodic review to dynamic, ongoing improvement that supports both institutional effectiveness and educational equity.

Moving forward, the success of AI-enhanced accreditation will depend on three commitments: continuous evaluation, deep stakeholder engagement, and policy frameworks that prioritize educational integrity over technological convenience. The responsibility now rests with today's institutions, educators, and accrediting bodies to lead this transformation with intentionality—ensuring that AI not only supports compliance but also strengthens the quality and fairness of teacher preparation worldwide.

Reflection Prompts—Chapter 7

The following prompts are designed to help educator preparation programs (EPPs), accreditation bodies, and faculty leaders critically engage with the strategic, ethical, and operational considerations presented in this chapter. These questions may be used for individual reflection, team discussions, or as part of institutional planning and professional development activities.

1. **Framework Adoption**—How could your institution apply elements from established ethical AI frameworks or accreditation governance models to strengthen and modernize its accreditation processes?

2. **Balancing AI and Human Judgment**—In what ways can AI's analytical capabilities enhance accreditation while ensuring that final decisions remain firmly rooted in faculty expertise?

3. **Equity Considerations**—How might AI tools unintentionally replicate inequities in accreditation, and what safeguards could be implemented to prevent this?

4. **Transparency Practices**—What steps could your institution take to ensure that AI-driven accreditation processes are transparent and understandable to all stakeholders?

5. **Governance Readiness**—Does your institution currently have clear governance structures for AI in accreditation? If not, what would be the first step in creating them?

6. **Ethical Risk Assessment**—How can your accreditation team identify and address ethical risks before adopting AI tools?

7. **Continuous Improvement**—How might AI be used not only for compliance but also as a driver of ongoing program improvement in teacher preparation?

8. **Stakeholder Engagement**—In what ways could faculty, students, and community members be engaged in co-designing AI-enhanced accreditation processes?

9. **Capacity-Building**—What professional development would be necessary to prepare faculty and administrators for effective, ethical use of AI in accreditation?

10. **Future Vision**—How do you envision the role of AI in accreditation evolving over the next decade, and what should your institution do now to prepare for that future?

Appendix A

Quick Reference Guide: Using AI Tools Under FERPA Council for the Accreditation of Educator Preparation (CAEP)

This guide provides practical guidance for using generative AI tools while maintaining compliance with the Family Educational Rights and Privacy Act (FERPA).

Key Reminder

FERPA protects any information that can identify a student.

AI should be used as a decision-support tool, not as a record-keeping or compliance system.

When uncertain, consult the institution's FERPA Officer before inputting data into AI systems.

Table A.1 "Do"s and "Don't"s of AI for Ethical Compliance

Do	Don't
Anonymize Data: Replace student names with codes (e.g., "Candidate A").	Upload Student Identifiers: Names, ID numbers, email addresses, or grades.
Use Aggregate Results: Summarize performance trends (e.g., "80% met standard").	Enter Identifiable Work: Lesson plans, assignments, or evaluations tied to specific students.
Draft with AI: Policies, rubrics, lesson plan templates, handbooks, accreditation reports.	Use AI for High-Stakes Decisions: Admissions, licensure, or final grading.
Generate Teaching Materials: Case studies, sample lessons, discussion prompts.	Store FERPA-Protected Records: Never upload to AI systems without IT/legal approval.
Use Institution-Approved Platforms: Prefer Enterprise/Team accounts with administrative controls.	Assume AI is Confidential: Temporary chats help, but FERPA protections still apply.
Apply Human Oversight: Treat AI outputs as drafts—final evaluative judgment rests with faculty.	

Reference List

Adorni, G., & Ponzini, D. (2024). Building a "conversational AI" syllabus for educator certification: A framework for integrating AI in educational practice. *ICERI2024 Proceedings*, Seville, Spain. https://library.iated.org/view/ADORNI2024BUI

Agarwal, R., Bjarnadottir, M., Rhue, L., Dugas, M., Crowley, K., Clark, J., & Gao, G. (2023). Addressing algorithmic bias and the perpetuation of health inequities: An AI bias aware framework. *Health Policy and Technology, 12*(1), 100702. https://doi.org/10.1016/j.hlpt.2022.100702

Akinwalere, S., & Ivanov, V. (2022). Artificial intelligence in higher education: Challenges and opportunities. *Border Crossing, 12*(1), 1–15. https://doi.org/10.33182/bc.v12i1.2015

Alexandrowicz, V. (2024). Artificial intelligence integration in teacher education: Navigating benefits, challenges, and transformative pedagogy. *Journal of Education and Learning, 13*(6), 346. https://doi.org/10.5539/jel.v13n6p346

Annuš, N. (2024). Education in the age of artificial intelligence. *TEM Journal, 13*(1), 404–413. https://doi.org/10.18421/TEM131-42

Azzam, T. (2023). Artificial intelligence and validity. *New Directions for Evaluation*, 2023, 85–95. https://doi.org/10.1002/ev.20565

Baidoo-Anu, D., & Owusu Ansah, L. (2023). Education in the era of generative artificial intelligence (AI): Understanding the potential benefits of ChatGPT in promoting teaching and learning. *Journal of AI, 7*(1), 52–62. https://doi.org/10.61969/jai.1337500

Baker, R. S., & Hawn, A. (2022). Algorithmic bias in education. *International Journal of Artificial Intelligence in Education, 32*, 1052–1092. https://doi.org/10.1007/s40593-021-00285-9

Bendermacher, G. W. G., oude Egbrink, M. G. A., Wolfhagen, I. H. A. P., & Dolmans, D. H. J. M. (2017). Unravelling quality culture in higher education: A realist review. *Higher Education, 73*(1), 39–60. https://doi.org/10.1007/s10734-015-9979-2

Bienkowski, M., Feng, M., & Means, B. (2012). Enhancing teaching and learning through educational data mining and learning analytics: An issue brief. *U.S. Department of Education.* https://tech.ed.gov/wp-content/uploads/2014/03/edm-la-brief.pdf

Bisoux, T. (2024, September 11). How can AI support your accreditation efforts? *Association to Advance Collegiate Schools of Business.* https://www.aacsb.edu/insights

Cayirtepe, Z., & Cizmeci Senel, F. (2022). Artificial intelligence-supported self-assessment systems in quality management. *International Journal for Quality in Health Care, 34*(2), mzac025. https://doi.org/10.1093/intqhc/mzac025

Cetin, G., Karatay, C., Kartal, E., Şahin, M., & Çiftçi, İ. (2024). Challenges with AI adoption in social sciences teaching. Istanbul University. https://www.researchgate.net/publication/388476069

Chu, A., & Sisson, A. (2024). Academic misconduct and best practices for conducting oral exams. *Napier Repository.* https://napier-repository.worktribe.com/output/3651029

Cooper, G., Tang, K. S., & Fitzgerald, A. (2025). Intersections of mind and machine: Navigating the nexus of artificial intelligence, science education, and the preparation of pre-service teachers. *Journal of Science Education and Technology 34*, 1255–1259. https://doi.org/10.1007/s10956-025-10200-9

Council for Higher Education Accreditation International Quality Group. (2025, February). Guiding principles for artificial intelligence in accreditation and recognition. *Council for Higher Education Accreditation.*

Council for the Accreditation of Educator Preparation. (2021). *CAEP advanced standards.* https://caepnet.org/advanced-standards/

Council for the Accreditation of Educator Preparation. (2022a). *CAEP initial standards.* https://caepnet.org/caep-standards/

Council for the Accreditation of Educator Preparation. (2022b). *CAEP accreditation handbook.* CAEP. https://caepnet.org/accreditation/caep-accreditation

Edwards, R. A., White, B. A. A., & Findyartini, A. (2025). Innovations in teaching and learning for health professions educators. *Frontiers in Medicine, 12*, 1611578. https://www.frontiersin.org/articles/10.3389/fmed.2025.1611578/full

Fernández-Sánchez, A., Lorenzo-Castiñeiras, J. J., & Sánchez-Bello, A. (2025). Navigating the future of pedagogy: The integration of AI tools in developing educational assessment rubrics. *European Journal of Education, 60*(1), e12826. https://doi.org/10.1111/ejed.12826

Ferrara, E. (2024). Fairness and bias in artificial intelligence: A brief survey of sources, impacts, and mitigation strategies. *Sci, 6*(1), 3. https://doi.org/10.3390/sci6010003

Floridi, L., & Cowls, J. (2019). A unified framework of five principles for AI in society. *Harvard Data Science Review*, 1(1), 1–14.

Harvey, Lee & Stensaker, Bjørn. (2008). Quality Culture: understandings, boundaries and linkages. *European Journal of Education*, 43. 427–442. 10.1111/j.1465-3435.2008.00367.x.

Hoke, T. (2025). Education for 21st-century learners. *Proceedings of the ICSDI 2024* (Vol. 2). https://books.google.com/books?hl=en&id=ApssEQAAQBAJ

Holmes, W., Bialik, M., & Fadel, C. (2019). Artificial intelligence in education: Promises and implications for teaching and learning. *Center for Curriculum Redesign*. https://curriculumredesign.org/wp-content/uploads/AIED-Book-Excerpt-CCR.pdf

Holmes, W., & Porayska-Pomsta, K. (2023). *The ethics of artificial intelligence in education*. Routledge. https://doi.org/10.4324/9780429329067

Ifenthaler, D., & Yau, J. Y.-K. (2020). Utilising learning analytics for study success: Reflections on current empirical findings. *Research and Practice in Technology Enhanced Learning, 15*(1), 1–13. https://doi.org/10.1007/s11423-020-09788-z

Johnson, N., Seaman, J., & Seaman, J. (2024). *The anticipated impact of artificial intelligence on US higher education: A national study. Online Learning, 28*(3), 9–33. https://doi.org/10.24059/olj.v28i3.4646

Kahlow, J. (2024). AI rubrics. *In The alchemy of assessment and evaluation*. Mavs Open Press. https://uta.pressbooks.pub/thealchemy/chapter/ai-rubrics/

Kasneci, E., Seegerer, S., Kühn, S., Kasneci, G., & Sessler, K. (2023). ChatGPT for good? On opportunities and challenges of large language models for education. *Learning and Individual Differences, 103*, 102274. https://doi.org/10.1016/j.lindif.2023.102274

Kelly, M. P., & Smith, M. H. (2024). How to think about integrating generative AI in professional military education. *Military Review*. https://www.armyupress.army.mil/Portals/7/military-review/Archives/English/Online-Exclusive/2024/Integrating-Generative-AI/Kelly-and-Smith-Generative-AI-UA.pdf

Krooi, M., Whittingham, J., & Beausaert, S. (2024). Introducing the 3P conceptual model of internal quality assurance in higher education: A systematic literature review. *Studies in Educational Evaluation, 82*, 101360. https://doi.org/10.1016/j.stueduc.2024.101360

Li, P., Zhang, S., Liu, Y., He, Y., Gao, J., & Wang, Y. (2023). *Making AI less "thirsty": Uncovering and addressing the secret water footprint of AI models*. arXiv preprint arXiv:2304.03271. https://arxiv.org/abs/2304.03271

Li, S., & Li, D. (2025). Research on personalized learning recommendation system. *Scalable Computing: Practice and Experience, 26*(1). https://scpe.org/index.php/scpe/article/view/3844

Masoumian Hosseini, S. T., Qayumi, K., Pourabbasi, A. (2025) Are we ready to integrate modern technologies into the medical curriculum for students a systematic review. *Discover Education 4*, 114. https://doi.org/10.1007/s44217-025-00521-7

Mhlanga, D. (2023). *The role of artificial intelligence in higher education quality assurance*. SSRN. https://doi.org/10.2139/ssrn.4354422

Morris, D. (2025). Artificial intelligence and accreditation: Balancing the human touch. *Teaching and Learning in Nursing, 20*(1), 5–7. https://doi.org/10.1016/j.teln.2024.11.026

Mustapha, S. (2024). The use of technology and artificial intelligence in legal education. *Fountain University Law Journal, 1*(2). http://www.fountainjournals.com/index.php/FULAJ/article/view/546

National Association of State Directors of Teacher Education and Certification. (2023). *Strategic plan 2024–2029*. https://cdn.ymaws

.com/www.nasdtec.net/resource/resmgr/strategic_plan/strategic
_plan_2023-10-20.pdf

NIU College Trade School Articles (2025). AI-driven innovations
in higher education accreditation and state approval. https://
www.niucollege.edu/ai-driven-innovations-in-higher-education
-accreditation-and-state-approval

Office of Educational Technology. (2023). Artificial intelligence and the
future of teaching and learning: Insights and recommendations.
U.S. Department of Education. https://www.ed.gov/sites/default/
files/ai-report.pdf

OpenAI. (2025). *ChatGPT* (July 15 version). https://chat.openai.com/
chat

Pearson, J., & Monaco, M. (2025). *Navigating AI in educator preparation:
Considerations for EPPs*. Council for the Accreditation of Educator
Preparation.

Pilz, K. F., Mahmood, Y., & Heim, L. (2025). AI's power requirements
under exponential growth: Extrapolating AI data center
power demand and assessing its potential impact on U.S.
competitiveness. *RAND Corporation*. https://www.rand.org/pubs/
research_reports/RRA3572-1.html

Popenici, S. A. D., & Kerr, S. (2017). Exploring the impact of artificial
intelligence on teaching and learning in higher education.
Research and Practice in Technology Enhanced Learning, 12(1), 1–13.
https://doi.org/10.1186/s41039-017-0062-8

Prinsloo, P., Slade, S., & Khalil, M. (2021). *Learning analytics: A primer*.
Commonwealth of Learning. https://www.researchgate.net/
publication/354271371

Renz, A., & Hilbig, R. (2020). Prerequisites for artificial intelligence in
further education: Identification of drivers, barriers, and business
models of educational technology companies. *International
Journal of Educational Technology in Higher Education, 17*(44).
https://doi.org/10.1186/s41239-020-00193-3

Robbins, J. (n.d.). *Accreditation and NCATE "paperless" review at EMU*.
Eastern Michigan University, College of Education Archives.
Retrieved August 28, 2025, from https://www.emich.edu/coe/
about/1991-2004.php

Salas-Pilco, S. Z., Xiao, K., & Hu, X. (2022). Artificial intelligence and learning analytics in teacher education: A systematic review. *Education Sciences, 12*(8), 569. https://doi.org/10.3390/educsci12080569

Sclater, N. (2017). *Learning analytics explained.* Routledge. https://doi.org/10.4324/9781315679563

Shepherd, C. (2025). *Generative AI misuse potential in cybersecurity education: A case study of a UK degree program.* arXiv preprint arXiv:2501.12883. https://arxiv.org/abs/2501.12883

Singleton, J. D. (2025). Artificial intelligence in higher education accreditation: Advancing quality, accessibility, and special education inclusion. *Teacher Education Faculty Publications* (10). https://arch.astate.edu/ebs-tedu-facpub/10

Southern Association of Colleges and Schools Commission on Colleges. (2024, December). *Artificial intelligence in accreditation: Guideline. SACSCOC Board of Trustees.*

Stensaker, B., Langfeldt, L., Borch, O. J., & Amdam, S. V. (2022). Bounded innovation or agency drift? Developments in quality assurance agencies in Europe. *Quality in Higher Education, 28*(2), 177–190.

Stoodley, P., Oomens, D., & Robinson, C. (2024). Deep learning: Integrating artificial intelligence into the sonography curriculum. *Sonography, 41*(2), 85–102. https://doi.org/10.1002/sono.12450

Susanti, A. D. D. (2025). Developing 21st-century skills in elementary school students through artificial intelligence. *Pedagogik Journal of Islamic Elementary School, 8*(1), 66–77. https://doi.org/10.24256/pijies.v8i1.6362

Tabish, S. A. (2024). *Health care management: Principles and practice.* Springer. https://www.academia.edu/download/118957117/My_Springer_Book.pdf

Triana, O. A. D., Portela, F. G., & Reina, F. A. (2024). Utilization of data governance as support for quality assurance in the systems engineering program at the Universidad Cooperativa de Colombia. *2024 IEEE VII International Congress on Information and Communication Technology.* https://doi.org/10.1109/AmITIC62658.2024.10747646

UNESCO. (2021). AI and education: Guidance for policy-makers. *United Nations Educational, Scientific and Cultural Organization.* https://unesdoc.unesco.org/ark:/48223/pf0000376709

U.S. Department of Education. (2023). Artificial intelligence and the future of teaching and learning: Insights and recommendations. *Office of Educational Technology*. https://tech.ed.gov/files/2023/05/AI-Report-2023.pdf

U.S. Department of Education. (2025). Title II technical assistance. *Title II Higher Education Act*. https://title2.ed.gov/Public/TA.aspx

Viberg, O., Mavroudi, A., Bälter, O., & Wasson, B. (2023). Teachers' trust in artificial intelligence: A large-scale international survey. *Computers & Education: Artificial Intelligence, 4*, 100167. https://doi.org/10.1016/j.caeai.2023.100167

Voiosu, A. M., & Gonçalves, T. C. (2024). Ethical AI in endoscopy education. *Endoscopy International Open, 12*(7), E837–E841. https://doi.org/10.1055/a-2232-9949

Wang, L., & Xing, S. (2024). A study on the influencing factors model of AI-E-TPACK for preservice teachers. *Artificial Intelligence for Education Symposium*. https://doi.org/10.1145/3700297.3700377

Wiggins, G., & McTighe, J. (2005). Understanding by design (Expanded 2nd ed.). *Association for Supervision and Curriculum Development*.

Williamson, B. (2019). Datafication of education. In H. Beetham & R. Sharpe (Eds.), *Rethinking pedagogy for a digital age* (3rd ed., pp. 268–284). Routledge. https://doi.org/10.4324/9781351252805-14

Williamson, B., & Eynon, R. (2020). Historical threads, missing links, and future directions in AI in education. *Learning, Media and Technology, 45*(3), 223–235. https://doi.org/10.1080/17439884.2020.1798995

Zawacki-Richter, O., Marín, V. I., Bond, M., & Gouverneur, F. (2019). Systematic review of research on artificial intelligence applications in higher education – Where are the educators? *International Journal of Educational Technology in Higher Education, 16*(1), 39. https://doi.org/10.1186/s41239-019-0171-0

Zhai, X., Chu, X., Chai, C.S., Jong, M.S., Istenič, A., Spector, M., Liu, J., Yuan, J., & Li, Y. (2021). A Review of Artificial Intelligence (AI) in Education from 2010 to 2020. *Complexity, 2021*(6), 1–18.

Index